ONE WEEK LOAN

Achieving QTS

Primary Science: Audit and Test
Assessing your knowledge and understanding

Third edition

John Sharp

Jenny Byrne

Learning Matters

First published in 2001 by Learning Matters Ltd.
Reprinted in 2002.
Second edition published in 2003.
Reprinted in 2003.
Reprinted in 2004.
Reprinted in 2005.
Reprinted in 2006.
Third edition published in 2007.
Reprinted in 2007 (twice).
Reprinted in 2008.
Reprinted in 2009.

© John Sharp and Jenny Byrne

British Library Cataloguing in Publication Data
A CIP record for this book is available from the British Library.

ISBN 978 1 84445 109 8

Cover design by Topics – The Creative Partnership
Text design by Code 5 Design Associates Ltd
Project Management by Deer Park Productions, Tavistock
Typeset by PDQ Typesetting Ltd, Newcastle-under-Lyme
Printed and bound in Great Britain by Bell & Bain Ltd, Glasgow

Learning Matters Ltd
33 Southernhay East
Exeter EX1 1NX
Tel: 01392 215560
info@learningmatters.co.uk
www.learningmatters.co.uk

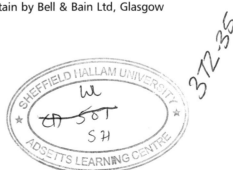

Contents

Introduction

About this book

This book has been written to support the subject knowledge learning of all primary trainee teachers on courses of Initial Teacher Training (ITT) in England and other parts of the UK where a secure subject knowledge and understanding of science is required for the award of Qualified Teacher Status (QTS). A secure subject knowledge and understanding of science is now widely acknowledged as a critical factor at every point in the complex process of planning, teaching and assessing science. The audit and test materials presented here will help you to identify your own strengths and weaknesses in science. As you revise, you can revisit these to help you monitor and evaluate your own progress towards QTS:

Part 1: Science background;
Part 2: Interest in science;
Part 3: Perceived competence and confidence in science;
Part 4: Science test;
Part 5: Answers to test questions;
Part 6: Targets for further development;
Part 7: Revision and further reading.

It is quite likely that you will be required to undertake further auditing and testing of your subject knowledge and understanding of science at the start of your own course of ITT. You may wish to retain the audit and test result details for your own records and use them to return to as and when necessary. Your ITT provider may also wish to use them for their own records.

While you may indeed find the process of auditing and testing your science subject knowledge particularly daunting, especially if you were last taught or thought about science several years ago, most people simply take it all in their stride and you should aim to do the same. Auditing and testing are simply two forms of assessment and you will be assessed in lots of different ways throughout your career in teaching, not just when you train. There is certainly nothing to worry about when auditing and testing yourself in the comfort of your own home. Your ITT provider will also take every step they can to help minimise the apparent stress of auditing and testing as they guide you towards your goal of becoming an effective and successful primary school teacher.

For trainees wishing to undertake some revision or who feel the need for a science study aid there are several excellent books written specifically for primary trainees with diverse backgrounds in science. Some of these are listed in Part 7. All are available from good booksellers. We, of course, would recommend *Primary Science: Knowledge and Understanding* (third edition) by Peacock et al. (2007) from the *Learning Matters Achieving QTS Series* (see References). Almost all of the test questions and diagrams here are drawn from this source. Similarly, we would also recommend *Primary Science: Teaching Theory and Practice* (third edition) by Sharp et al. (2007).

The Standards for Qualified Teacher Status (2007)

A statutory framework for the career-long professional development of teachers has been designed by the Training and Development Agency for Schools (TDA). Within this wider framework, national standards for Qualified Teacher Status (QTS) are specified which trainee teachers must meet if they are to be awarded QTS.

These include, as aspects of professional knowledge and understanding, the requirements for trainee teachers to know and understand the *National Curriculum for Science* and to have a secure knowledge and understanding of the science curriculum as appropriate to the age range for which they are trained. The Primary National Strategy (PNS) is a non-statutory framework that offers guidance which allows teachers to take control of their own curriculum and be innovative. With respect to science this will mean offering pupils enjoyable and creative learning opportunities which may be integrated with other subject areas. A high level of science subject knowledge is an essential aspect of teaching in this manner. The audit and test materials in this book include many aspects of the specific science subject knowledge which you will need to know and understand in order to plan, teach and assess within these frameworks.

In terms of the professional skills set out in the Standards, it is vital that your subject knowledge is sufficiently secure for you to feel confident in teaching and assessing children's learning. Strong subject knowledge will enable you to understand the concepts you teach so that you can explain them effectively and offer examples, and help your pupils to investigate them and develop their own understandings. Strong subject knowledge will enable you to identify specifically what your pupils can do, and what they need to learn next. It will help you devise effective questions and provide feedback to move learning on.

The Standards also require you to show that you are beginning to address your personal professional development through taking steps to identify and meet your own professional needs. This book, by helping you to identify particular areas of subject knowledge for further study, has been designed to help you do this.

The subject content of science includes:

- **the nature of science;**
- **the process of planning, carrying out and evaluating scientific investigations;**
- **the methods employed in scientific investigation;**
- **the need for clear and precise forms of communication;**
- **health and safety requirements and how to implement them;**
- **life processes (including functioning of organisms, continuity and change, and ecosystems);**
- **materials and their properties (including materials and particle theory and the conservation of mass);**
- **physical processes (including electricity and magnetism, energy, forces and motion, light, sound, the Earth and beyond).**

The audit materials presented here will introduce you to all of the content items listed above in detail. You will also have the opportunity to test your knowledge and understanding, but only in some.

Science: the statutory framework

The National Curriculum for England (1999)

Schools have a statutory duty to teach the National Curriculum, which was introduced in 1989. It is organised on the basis of four Key Stages, of which Key Stage 1 for 5-7 year-olds (Years 1 and 2) and Key Stage 2 for 7-11 year-olds (Years 3-6) cover the primary years. The *National Curriculum* for each Key Stage includes Programmes of Study which set out the science that children should be taught, and Attainment Targets, a series of level descriptions which provide a basis for making judgements about pupils' performance. A brief summary of the primary science Programmes of Study is as follows:

- Sc1: Scientific enquiry (ideas and evidence in science; investigative skills);
- Sc2: Life processes and living things (life processes; humans and other animals; green plants; variation and classification; living things in their environment);
- Sc3: Materials and their properties (grouping materials; changing materials; separating mixtures of materials – Key Stage 2 only);
- Sc4: Physical processes (electricity; forces and motion; light and sound; the Earth and beyond – Key Stage 2 only).

Science in the National Curriculum is supported by an exemplar Scheme of Work for Science at Key Stages 1 and 2 (see References). While there is no statutory requirement for schools to use the Scheme of Work for Science at Key Stages 1 and 2, many are now adapting it to suit their own needs.

The Foundation Stage

The scope of the National Curriculum was extended in 2002 to incorporate the Foundation Stage, introduced two years earlier as a distinct stage of education for children aged from 3 to 5. The Early Years curriculum, set out in *Curriculum Guidance for the Foundation Stage* (2000), covers six broad areas of learning, including 'Knowledge and understanding of the world'. Statutory early learning goals describe what children are expected to achieve in these areas by the end of the Reception year, and provide the basis for the Early Years curriculum. In Autumn 2008, the Foundation Stage becomes part of the new Early Years Foundation Stage, covering care, learning and development for children in all early years settings from birth to the age of five.

References

DfEE/QCA (1999) *Science: the National Curriculum for England*. London: HMSO. (Also available online at www.nc.uk.net)

DfEE/QCA (2000) *Curriculum Guidance for the Foundation Stage*. London: QCA.

Sharp, J., Peacock, G., Johnsey, R., Simon, S., and Smith, R. (2007) *Primary Science: Teaching Theory and Practice*. (3rd ed.) Exeter: Learning Matters.

Peacock, G., Sharp, J., Johnsey, R., and Wright, D. (2007) *Primary Science: Knowledge and Understanding*. (3rd ed.) Exeter: Learning Matters.

QCA/DfEE (1998 with amendments 2000) *Science: a Scheme of Work for Key Stages 1 and 2*. London: QCA. (Also available online at www.qca.org.uk and www.standards.dfes.gov.uk/schemes)

TDA (2007) *Standards for the recommendation of Qualified Teacher Status*. London: TDA. (Available online at http://www.tda.gov.uk/)

Part 1: Science background

Provide as many background details as you can. Don't worry if it looks a bit 'blank' in places, you won't be alone. Unless you're a prospective science specialist what else would you expect?

▶ **personal details**

Name

Date of birth

Year(s) of course

Subject specialism

Elected Key Stage

▶ **science qualifications**

GCSE/O level (equivalent)

Date taken

Grade(s)

GCE A level (equivalent)

Date taken

Grade(s)

▶ **science degree**

Subject

Year of graduation

Class of degree

Other science courses

▶ **other** (e.g. work related)

Part 2: Interest in science

A positive attitude towards science will help you to learn and teach it well, whether it's your favourite subject or not. Be honest with yourself and think carefully about your responses below. It is possible, for example, that you might have a healthy interest in science even if you don't think you know too much about it right now.

Circle as appropriate using the key provided.

1 = I am very interested in science.
2 = I am interested in science.
3 = I am uncertain about my interest in science.
4 = I am not interested in science.

Interest   **1**   **2**   **3**   **4**

A 1 or a 2 is fantastic, a 3 encouraging, a 4 – well, science isn't everybody's thing. Reflect critically on your attitude towards science, positive or negative, and use the space below to comment further. Can you identify the experiences which gave rise to your interest or lack of it?

experiences statement

Part 3: Perceived competence and confidence in science

It is entirely possible that as you respond to the following sections you might notice that you feel quite competent in an area of science, or even a 'strand' within it, but lack the confidence to teach it. Competence and confidence are clearly quite different things. By the end of your training you will feel better about both.

Competence

There are rather a lot of areas within the self-audit and you will need some time to read through and complete this part thoroughly. The 'strands' are reproduced here to introduce you to requirements. You do not need to know about or feel competent with everything listed here right now. There will be plenty of time for this later.

Please respond to the following statements using the key provided.

1 = **Very good. Existing competence perceived as *exceeding* the requirements.**

2 = **Good. Existing competence perceived as *meeting* the requirements *comfortably*.**

3 = **Adequate. Existing competence perceived as *meeting* the requirements but *some* uncertainties still exist.**

4 = **Not good. Existing competence perceived as *not meeting* the requirements.**

Nature of science

To underpin and to support the effective teaching of primary science you should know and understand something of the nature of science, for example:

	1	**2**	**3**	**4**
• science is a way of making sense of natural phenomena and as such involves the interaction of an existing body of knowledge with the 'discovery' of new evidence, leading to a re-interpretation or explanation of phenomena and processes	1	2	3	4
• scientific knowledge and explanations may change as new evidence is collected and thinking is challenged	1	2	3	4
• science is a co-operative activity which involves a community of scientists and others in developing more powerful ways of understanding the natural world	1	2	3	4
• science does not explain every phenomenon	1	2	3	4
• scientific knowledge and understanding can be used in solving a range of problems but the available scientific evidence is often limited, and its application to everyday problems often entails ethical or moral questions	1	2	3	4
• science has played a part in many of the things that you use	1	2	3	4

The process of planning, carrying out and evaluating scientific investigations

To underpin and to support the effective teaching of primary science you should know and understand something of the ways of planning, carrying out and evaluating scientific investigations, for example:

	1	2	3	4
• the fact that not all questions can be investigated practically	1	2	3	4
• how to construct questions that can be investigated, including considering the distinction between a guess, a prediction and a hypothesis	1	2	3	4
• how to plan investigations appropriate to the question asked, the resources available and the context in which they are carried out	1	2	3	4
• the nature of variables including: identification of categoric, independent and dependent variables, and recognition of discrete and continuous variables	1	2	3	4
• the structure and use of controlled experiments, taking into account all the relevant variables to allow valid comparison of different sets of data	1	2	3	4
• the ways in which sample size can be selected, how this will influence the outcomes of investigation and how this can be recognised when findings are interpreted	1	2	3	4
• the need to plan investigations so as to use the most appropriate scientific methods for the collection, analysis and interpretation of evidence	1	2	3	4
• possible reasons for experimental findings not supporting accepted scientific evidence, including: extent of available evidence, natural variation in measurements, limitations in resources and experimental design	1	2	3	4
• the fact that outcomes of an investigation should be considered in the light of the original question and the wider body of available and relevant scientific evidence	1	2	3	4

The methods employed in scientific investigations and how to use them to collect, record, analyse and interpret evidence

To underpin and to support the effective teaching of primary science you should know and understand something of the methods employed in scientific investigation and how to use them in order to collect, record, analyse and interpret evidence, for example:

	1	2	3	4
• the variety of ways to collect evidence including techniques for observing, measuring, testing and controlling variables, carrying out surveys, sampling, using models and interrogating secondary sources	1	2	3	4

- the importance of selecting and using equipment correctly in order to gather evidence at the required level of detail 1 2 3 4

- the need for accuracy and precision in observations of measurements, in the replication of readings, in the control of variables and in the acknowledgement of sources of evidence in order to establish the reproducibility, reliability and validity of evidence 1 2 3 4

- the appropriate units, including SI units, which should be used to quantify the different types of measurements required 1 2 3 4

- the need to record the relevant evidence accurately and, where appropriate at suitable time intervals, using appropriate techniques, including tables, histograms, graphs or electronic devices 1 2 3 4

- the different ways in which evidence can be analysed such as looking for patterns and trends using simple mathematical devices, e.g. means, scattergrams, recognising that the form of analysis chosen should be matched to the type of evidence available 1 2 3 4

- the different ways in which objects and organisms can be identified and classified, including the construction and use of keys 1 2 3 4

The need for clear and precise forms of communication in science

To underpin and to support the effective teaching of primary science you should know and understand something of the need for clear and precise forms of communication in science, for example:

1 2 3 4

- correct scientific terminology for phenomena, events and processes 1 2 3 4

- the accepted scientific terminology, forms of representation, symbols and conventions 1 2 3 4

- a wide range of methods, including diagrams, drawings, graphs, tables and charts, to record and present information in an appropriate and systematic manner 1 2 3 4

Health and safety requirements and how to implement them

To underpin and to support the effective teaching of primary science you should know and understand something of health and safety requirements and how to implement them, for example:

1 2 3 4

- the major legal requirements for health and safety, including restrictions on keeping living things in the classroom 1 2 3 4

9

- the fact that every activity involves an element of risk which should be assessed and allowed for in planning and organising it   1 2 3 4
- the accepted actions and procedures in the event of an accident   1 2 3 4

Life processes

To underpin and to support the effective teaching of primary science you should know and understand something of life processes and living things, for example:

a) functioning of organisms   **1 2 3 4**

- differences between things that are living and things that have never been alive   1 2 3 4
- that organisms have the potential to carry out the life processes of nutrition, movement, growth, reproduction, respiration, sensitivity and excretion   1 2 3 4
- that humans have senses which enable them to be aware of the world around them   1 2 3 4
- naming the main external parts of the human body   1 2 3 4
- the functions of teeth and the importance of dental care   1 2 3 4
- a simple model of the structure of the heart and how it acts as a pump   1 2 3 4
- how blood circulates in the body through arteries and veins   1 2 3 4
- the effect of exercise and rest on pulse rate   1 2 3 4
- that humans have skeletons and muscles to support their bodies and to help them move   1 2 3 4
- the main stages of the human life cycle   1 2 3 4
- the functions of nutrition, circulation, movement, growth and reproduction in humans   1 2 3 4
- how to recognise and name the leaf, flower, stem and root of flowering plants   1 2 3 4
- that plant growth is affected by the availability of light and water, and by temperature   1 2 3 4
- that plants need light to produce food for growth, and the importance of the leaf in this process   1 2 3 4
- that the root anchors the plant, and that water and nutrients are taken in through the root and transported through the stem to other parts of the plant   1 2 3 4
- about the life cycle of flowering plants, including pollination, seed production, seed dispersal and germination   1 2 3 4
- how the various tissues and organs of a multi-cellular organism carry out specialised functions   1 2 3 4
- how the health of an organism can be affected by a range of factors, for example, in humans, drugs, exercise and other physical, mental and environmental factors   1 2 3 4

- that health can be threatened by a variety of agents   1   2   3   4
- that organisms have various ways of keeping themselves healthy   1   2   3   4
- that food is needed for activity and for growth, and that an adequate and varied diet is needed to keep healthy   1   2   3   4
- that most organisms are made up of cells and almost all cells have a nucleus which controls their activities   1   2   3   4

b) continuity and change   **1   2   3   4**

- reproduction is necessary for a completed life cycle   1   2   3   4
- individual organisms eventually die   1   2   3   4
- the principal agent controlling the characteristics and working of cells and organisms is their genetic material, DNA   1   2   3   4
- reproduction results in DNA from the parent or parents being passed on to future generations   1   2   3   4
- before reproduction, the genetic material of an organism is replicated   1   2   3   4
- mutations may occur during the process of DNA replication and during sexual reproduction, and genetic material will inevitably be recombined, both of which will cause variation in the offspring. In asexual reproduction (cloning) the amount of variation is characteristically very small and the offspring look exactly like the parent   1   2   3   4
- most biologists believe that variation caused by genetic mutation and recombination, coupled with interaction between organisms and their environment, leads to natural selection and evolutionary change   1   2   3   4
- a species is a group of organisms which can interbreed to produce fertile offspring   1   2   3   4
- there is variation within any species   1   2   3   4
- how to recognise similarities and differences between individuals   1   2   3   4
- that living things can be grouped according to observable similarities and differences and identified using keys   1   2   3   4

c) ecosystems   **1   2   3   4**

- a diversity of organisms exist, and include bacteria, fungi, plants and animals   1   2   3   4
- a diversity of organisms is found in most habitats   1   2   3   4
- the organisms, including humans, in an ecosystem interact with each other and with the physical aspects of the environment   1   2   3   4
- that food chains show feeding relationships in an ecosystem   1   2   3   4
- that nearly all food chains start with green plants   1   2   3   4
- micro-organisms are widely distributed   1   2   3   4
- humans affect the environment in various ways   1   2   3   4

Materials and their properties

To underpin and to support the effective teaching of primary science you should know and understand something of materials, their structure and their properties, for example:

a) materials	1	2	3	4
• the types of particles that make up all materials include atoms, protons, neutrons and electrons	1	2	3	4
• there are about 100 elements which join together in different combinations to make up all biological and other materials	1	2	3	4
• when atoms of different elements combine, the resulting material is a compound	1	2	3	4
• atoms can be held together in different ways	1	2	3	4
• the properties of a compound depend on the way in which the particles making it up are arranged and held together, such as in molecules and giant structures	1	2	3	4
• in chemical reactions new substances are formed	1	2	3	4
• physical changes involve changes in the arrangement and spacing of particles but no new substances are formed	1	2	3	4
• that some changes can be reversed and some cannot	1	2	3	4
• the properties of materials can often be predicted from a knowledge of their structures, and vice versa, but can also depend on their shape and size	1	2	3	4
• that materials are chosen for specific uses on the basis of their properties	1	2	3	4
• that some materials are better thermal insulators than others	1	2	3	4
• that some materials are better electrical conductors than others	1	2	3	4
• that mixtures of materials can be separated in a variety of different ways	1	2	3	4
• how to describe and group rocks and soils on the basis of characteristics, including appearance, texture and permeability	1	2	3	4
• most materials can exist as solid, liquid and gas, depending on conditions	1	2	3	4
• changes of state can be brought about by transferring energy	1	2	3	4

b) particle theory and the conservation of mass	1	2	3	4
• finely divided substances still contain many atoms and molecules	1	2	3	4
• the movement of particles explains the properties of solids, liquids and changes such as dissolving, melting and evaporating	1	2	3	4
• during chemical changes bonds joining atoms together are broken and new bonds are formed	1	2	3	4
• mass is conserved in physical and chemical changes	1	2	3	4

Physical processes

To underpin and to support the effective teaching of primary science you should know and understand something of physical processes, for example:

a) electricity and magnetism	1	2	3	4
• all matter is made up of particles which include electrons – these carry a negative charge	1	2	3	4
• in good conductors, such as copper, a small proportion of electrons (so called 'free electrons') can move easily; in poor conductors, like wood, movement is very difficult	1	2	3	4
• 'resistance' (measured in ohms) is a measure of the difficulty of flow of electrons in the material	1	2	3	4
• when a cell (or battery) is attached to a circuit, it provides a 'push' which causes electrons to move in one direction around the circuit; this movement (flow) of electrons is called current (measured in amps)	1	2	3	4
• current is not consumed and is the same in all parts of a simple series circuit	1	2	3	4
• voltage (measured in volts) is a measure of the energy per unit charge and this might be considered as driving the current	1	2	3	4
• energy (measured in joules) stored in a battery is transferred to the circuit as the battery is used	1	2	3	4
• the power (measured in watts) of a device such as a bulb or motor is the rate at which energy is transferred to the device	1	2	3	4
• as moving electrons collide with fixed atoms in a circuit they make the atoms vibrate more; this vibration causes components such as bulb filaments to get hot and emit light	1	2	3	4
• a circuit including its components can be represented by standard symbols in circuit diagrams	1	2	3	4
• how to construct simple circuits involving batteries, wires, bulbs and buzzers on the basis of drawings and diagrams	1	2	3	4
• that many everyday appliances use electricity	1	2	3	4
• magnets have poles; like poles repel, unlike poles attract; the pole that points northwards is the north-seeking pole	1	2	3	4
• magnetism can act over a distance, so magnets can exert forces on objects with which they are not in contact	1	2	3	4
• a current flowing through a conductor produces a magnetic effect	1	2	3	4

b) energy	1	2	3	4
• there is a distinction between energy and force	1	2	3	4
• there is a distinction between energy and fuel	1	2	3	4
• particular fuels can be used in the generation of electricity	1	2	3	4

- transfer of energy is not confined to physics; it is important in chemical and biological processes too

  1   2   3   4

- although energy is always conserved it may be dissipated, reducing its availability as a resource

  1   2   3   4

c) forces and motion

1   2   3   4

- that both pushes and pulls are examples of forces

  1   2   3   4

- when an object is stationary or moving at a steady speed in a straight line, the forces acting on it are balanced

  1   2   3   4

- balanced forces produce no change in the movement of an object or shape of an object whereas unbalanced forces acting on an object can change its motion or its shape

  1   2   3   4

- the change in movement and/or shape of an object depends on the magnitude and direction of the force acting on it

  1   2   3   4

- forces such as (solid) friction, air resistance and water resistance oppose the relative motion between an object and what it is touching

  1   2   3   4

- in most situations there are forces such as friction retarding the motion of objects and so a driving force is needed to keep them moving at a steady speed

  1   2   3   4

- frictional forces between surfaces can also enable motion, e.g. by opposing the relative movement between shoe and floor or tyre and road

  1   2   3   4

- that when springs and elastic bands are stretched they exert a force on whatever is stretching them

  1   2   3   4

- that when springs are compressed they exert a force on whatever is compressing them

  1   2   3   4

- the SI unit in which forces are measured is the newton

  1   2   3   4

- the mass of an object is the amount of matter in it; mass is measured in grams and kilograms

  1   2   3   4

- gravitational attraction exists between all objects; this depends on the masses of the respective objects and how far apart they are

  1   2   3   4

- the weight of an object is a force measured in newtons, caused by the gravitational attraction between the Earth and the object and directed towards the centre of the Earth

  1   2   3   4

- a specific object will have the same mass on the Earth and on the Moon because it contains the same amount of matter

  1   2   3   4

- an object will weigh more on the Earth than on the Moon because the Earth is more massive and exerts greater gravitational attraction than the Moon

  1   2   3   4

- objects of different mass dropped at the same instant from the same point will land at the same time unless the air resistance is different

  1   2   3   4

- the relationship between speed, distance and time and the distinction between speed and acceleration

  1   2   3   4

d) light

	1	2	3	4
• light travels from a source	1	2	3	4
• light travels in a straight line unless something prevents it from doing so, for example, reflection or scattering, and that this can be used to explain the formation of shadows	1	2	3	4
• light can differ in intensity and wavelength	1	2	3	4
• the distinction between reflection and scattering and how images are formed in a mirror	1	2	3	4
• the colour of an object depends on the wavelength of light that it scatters, e.g. a black object scatters little light and absorbs light of all visual wavelengths; a green object scatters more green light than other colours which it absorbs more	1	2	3	4
• objects are seen when light is emitted or reflected from them and enters the eye through the pupil, causing the retina to send messages, carried by nerves, to the brain	1	2	3	4

e) sound

	1	2	3	4
• there are many kinds of sound and many sources of sound	1	2	3	4
• sounds are made when objects vibrate but vibrations are not always directly visible	1	2	3	4
• sound travels through a medium from a vibrating source	1	2	3	4
• sound waves can differ in amplitude and frequency and this leads to differences in loudness and pitch respectively	1	2	3	4
• sounds are heard when vibrations from an object enter the ears causing the eardrums to vibrate and impulses to be carried to the brain	1	2	3	4

f) the Earth and beyond

	1	2	3	4
• the Universe includes galaxies which include stars	1	2	3	4
• the Sun is one star in our galaxy and is at the centre of the Solar System				
• the order of the planets in our Solar System, their major features and relative distances from the Sun which they orbit	1	2	3	4
• that the Sun, the Earth and the Moon are approximately spherical	1	2	3	4
• the explanation of day and night and the evidence for it	1	2	3	4
• the explanations for the phases of the Moon and eclipses	1	2	3	4
• the explanations for the seasons and length of year	1	2	3	4
• that the position of the Sun appears to change during the day, and how shadows change as this happens	1	2	3	4

Making sense of your perceived competence

Look back over your **perceived competency** grades. Summarise each area in the following table by looking at the distribution of responses. In Physical processes, for example, say you ticked lots of 2s, 3s and 4s but no 1s, you should fill in your Range as 2s to 4s. Say also that you ticked more 3s than anything else, you should fill in your Mode, the most frequently occurring response, as mostly 3s.

	range	mode
Nature of science	_____	_____
Scientific investigation (ways)	_____	_____
Scientific investigation (methods)	_____	_____
Communication	_____	_____
Health and safety	_____	_____
Life processes	_____	_____
Materials and their properties	_____	_____
Physical processes	_____	_____

Mostly 1s   Areas summarised as mostly 1s suggest that most competency requirements are exceeded. Your perceived competence would place you at a level beyond that of a non-science specialist. Well done.

Mostly 2s   Areas summarised as mostly 2s suggest that most competency requirements are met comfortably. Some attention is necessary locally, certainly in the weaker elements. Your perceived competence places you at a level about that of a non-science specialist. With this sort of profile you probably have little to worry about.

Mostly 3s   Areas summarised as mostly 3s suggest that most competency requirements are met adequately. However, attention is necessary throughout. Your perceived competence places you at a level best described as approaching that specified for a non-science specialist. You're probably in good company and with a little effort you'll be up there with the best of them.

Mostly 4s   Areas summarised as mostly 4s suggest that most competency requirements are hardly being met at all, but remember, you only have to get there by the end of your training – not before! Given the nature of the requirements, a profile like this is not surprising, it wouldn't concern us at this stage so don't let it concern you.

Confidence

Examine the Programmes of Study for Key Stages 1 and 2 in the National Science Curriculum below carefully. Overall, how would you describe your confidence in terms of **teaching** them?

Please respond using the key provided.

1 = Very good. Might even feel happy to support colleagues!

2 = Good. Further professional development required in some aspects.

3 = Adequate. Further professional development required in most aspects.

4 = Not good. Further professional development essential in all aspects.

Sc1 Scientific enquiry

	1	2	3	4
• ideas and evidence in science	1	2	3	4
• investigative skills (planning, obtaining and presenting evidence, considering evidence and evaluating)	1	2	3	4

Sc2 Life processes and living things

	1	2	3	4
• life processes	1	2	3	4
• humans and other animals	1	2	3	4
• green plants	1	2	3	4
• variation and classification	1	2	3	4
• living things in the environment	1	2	3	4

Sc3 Materials and their properties

	1	2	3	4
• grouping and classifying materials	1	2	3	4
• changing materials	1	2	3	4
• separating mixtures of materials (KS2 only)	1	2	3	4

Sc4 Physical processes

	1	2	3	4
• electricity	1	2	3	4
• forces and motion	1	2	3	4
• light and sound	1	2	3	4
• the Earth and beyond (KS2 only)	1	2	3	4

Making sense of your perceived confidence

1s and 2s are fantastic – what's kept you away from the profession for so long! 3s are encouraging and we would imagine that many people would have this sort of profile. If you ticked any 4s, don't worry. You are being very honest with yourself and that is good. If you really felt so confident about teaching science now there wouldn't be any point in training you to do it, would there?

Reflect critically on your perceived confidence about teaching science and use the space below to comment further. Can you identify the 'source' of your confidence or the 'source' of your lack of it?

confidence statement

Part 4: Science test

Your own perception of competence and confidence is one thing, but how would you do if actually put to the test? As always, it doesn't matter how well or how badly you test now, you will have lots of time to make up for the science you've forgotten or simply never knew in the first place. The following pages explore your knowledge and understanding in many key areas of primary science using a variety of established test techniques. Take as long as you like and try not to cheat too much by looking at the answers! The marking system is fairly straightforward and easy to use (as it is impossible to monitor, 1 mark for every correct answer!).

Life processes

Functioning of organisms: green plants

1 Match the labels below with parts **A** to **H** shown in the diagram of the flowering plant.

leaf
root system
flower
lateral root
root hair
stem
shoot system
tap root

[8 MARKS]

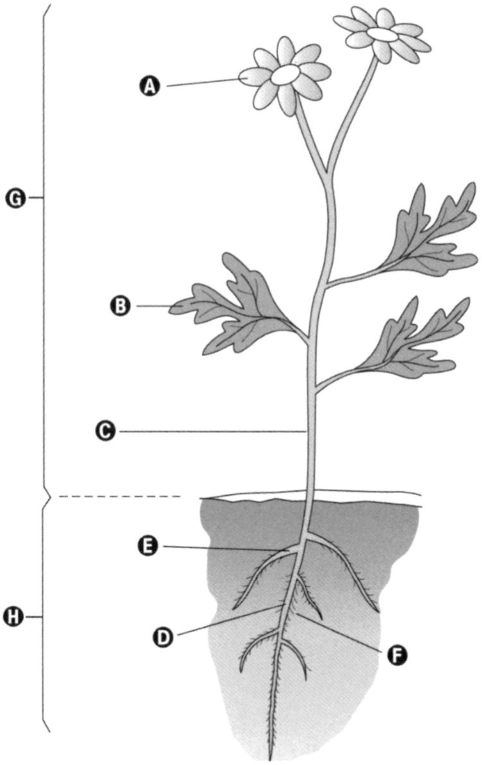

Complete the following sentences by inserting the most appropriate words:

Roots _____ plants firmly in the ground. They are also responsible for the uptake of _____ and _____ from the soil. Stems hold plants upright, spread out leaves for _____ and elevate flowers for _____ . Most leaves are green due to the presence of _____ . Flowers are the structures of most plants which are responsible for _____.

[7 MARKS]

2 In the diagram of the flower section shown, label the parts **A** to **H**.

anther
sepal
receptacle
style
petal
ovary with ovules
filament
stigma

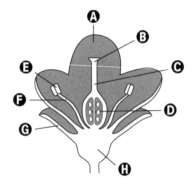

[8 MARKS]

Complete the following sentences by inserting the most appropriate words:

Flowers usually consist of five main elements (though these are not always present or immediately obvious): often brightly coloured and scented petals which attract _____ , papery sepals which _____ the flower in bud, male and female reproductive organs which work together to ensure the _____ of each species, and a receptacle which _____ the weight of everything.

[4 MARKS]

3 The male reproductive organs or stamen of a flowering plant includes:

(a) petals, sepals and a receptacle.
(b) the stigma, style and ovary.
(c) the anther and filament.   [1 MARK]

4 The female reproductive organs or carpel of a flowering plant include:

(a) the stigma, style and ovary.
(b) the anther and filament.
(c) petals, sepals and a receptacle.   [1 MARK]

5 In the diagram of the leaf section shown, label the parts **A** to **H**.

upper epidermal cells
spongy mesophyll cells
lower epidermal cells
waxy cuticle
guard cell
palisade mesophyll cells
'vein' (phloem and xylem vessels)
stoma

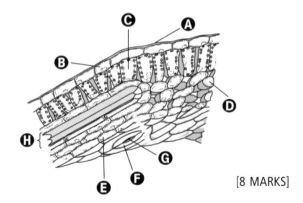

[8 MARKS]

Complete the following sentences by inserting the most appropriate words:

The leaves of many plants are large and _____ in order to trap sunlight and to make the process of photo-synthesis particularly efficient. A cross-section through a leaf blade or _____ reveals several layers including one consisting of palisade cells within the palisade mesophyll where most photosynthesis takes place. The rate of photosynthesis is affected by several factors including _____ intensity, air _____ , the concentration of _____ in the atmosphere, and _____ availability.

[6 MARKS]

6 Green plants are capable of making their own food in any of their green tissues by photosynthesis. Living organisms capable of doing this are referred to as:

(a) heterotrophs.
(b) autotrophs.
(c) rhizomes. [1 MARK]

7 Rearrange the following items to write out a word equation for photosynthesis:

energy in sunlight
glucose
carbon dioxide
oxygen
chlorophyll
water [3 MARKS]

8 In the diagram of the generalised plant cell (green tissue) shown, label the parts **A** to **H**.

chloroplast with chlorophyll
cellulose cell wall
nucleus
ribosome
cell membrane
cytoplasm
mitochondrion
sap-filled vacuole

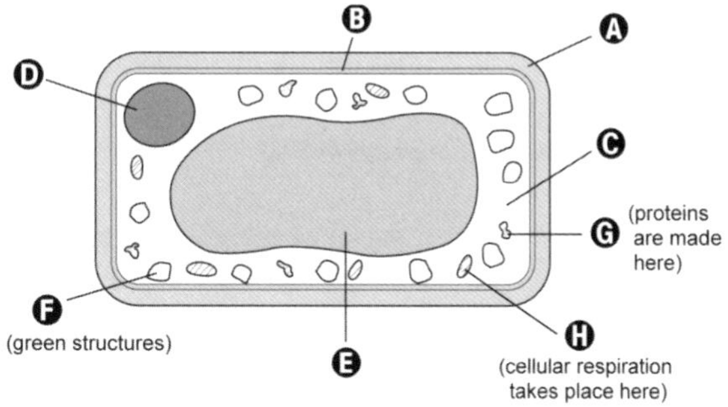

D

B

A

C

G (proteins are made here)

F (green structures)

E

H (cellular respiration takes place here)

[8 MARKS]

Complete the following sentences by inserting the most appropriate words:

The nucleus contains the plant cell's genetic material or _____ which ultimately determines what type of cell it is and controls what it does. The genetic material also has the ability to reproduce itself in a process known as _____ . This is important during cell division as plants _____ . Chloroplasts contain the green pigment chlorophyll, an important _____ responsible for bringing about photosynthesis.

[4 MARKS]

9 Plants are made from cells. Draw lines which match the specialised cell types on the left to their main function on the right.

root hair cells	form vessels which conduct simple sugars in sap
guard cells	carry out most photosynthesis in leaves
phloem cells	take up water and dissolved minerals from soil
xylem cells	form vessels which conduct water and dissolved minerals
palisade cells	allow various gases to move into and out of leaves

[5 MARKS]

10 Plants display certain characteristics which demonstrate that they are alive and carry out certain life processes in order to stay alive. These include:

(a) movement, growth and reproduction.
(b) respiration, sensitivity, excretion and nutrition.
(c) all of the above.   [1 MARK]

11 The reproductive cycle of a flowering plant proceeds in five well defined stages. Draw lines which match the reproductive stages on the left to the description which fits best on the right.

pollination	development of embryo plant
fertilisation	the transfer of pollen from anther to stigma
seed formation	scattering mechanism which helps avoid competition
seed dispersal	appearance of new root and shoot systems
germination	nuclei of male and female sex cells meet and fuse

[5 MARKS]

12 The common causes of ill health in plants include:

(a) mineral deficiencies.
(b) invertebrate organisms and plant pathogens.
(c) all of the above.   [1 MARK]

13 Modern classifications of living organisms within the plant kingdom recognise six main phyla as shown. Assign each of the plant groups below to its correct phylum.

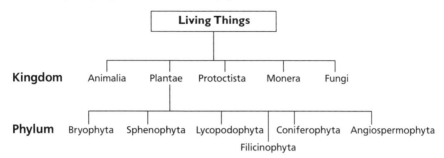

horsetails
ferns
flowering plants
mosses and liverworts
club mosses
conifers [6 MARKS]

14 The two classes of flowering plants, the most advanced and dominant forms of vegetation on Earth, are commonly referred to as:

(a) monocots and dicots.
(b) prokaryotes and eukaryotes.
(c) auxins and gibberellins. [1 MARK]

Functioning of organisms: humans and other animals

1 In the diagram of the skeleton shown on page 24, label the bones **A** to **R**.

patella
cranium
mandible
scapula
sacrum, ilium and coccyx (bones of the pelvis)
maxilla
radius
femur
carpals, metacarpals and phalanges (bones of the hand)
fibula
sternum
clavicle
humerus
vertebra
rib
ulna
tibia
tarsals, metatarsals and phalanges (bones of the foot) [18 MARKS]

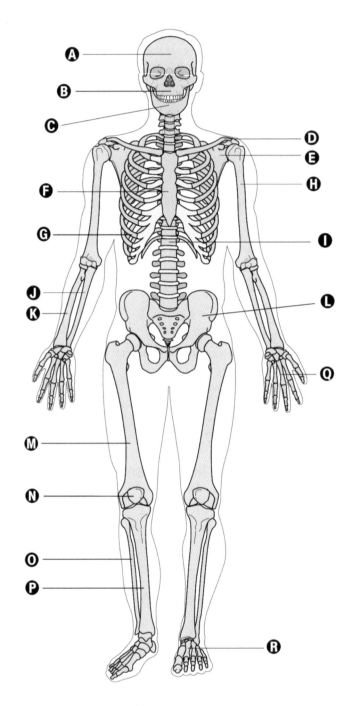

Complete the following sentences by inserting the most appropriate words:

The human skeleton _____ vital organs. It provides a framework which supports the _____ of individuals and, with the help of muscles, allows humans to _____ upright. The human skeleton also provides attachment for _____ and _____ allowing free movements to take place across joints.

[5 MARKS]

2 How many bones would you expect to find in the skeleton of an average human adult:

(a) **103?**
(b) **206?**
(c) **602?**   [1 MARK]

3 Bone is a living tissue. True or false?
                                                                                                      [1 MARK]

4 With reference to the diagram of the human muscular system shown:

(a) **What would you expect to happen as the biceps muscles of the arms contract?**
(b) **What would you expect to happen as the triceps muscles of the arms contract?**
(c) **Which is the largest muscle in the human body?**
(d) **Where might you expect to find the body's smallest muscles?**
(e) **The skeletal muscles of the human body shown are the most obvious and powerful muscles
    and are responsible for most of the body's voluntary movements. True or false?**
                                                                                                      [5 MARKS]

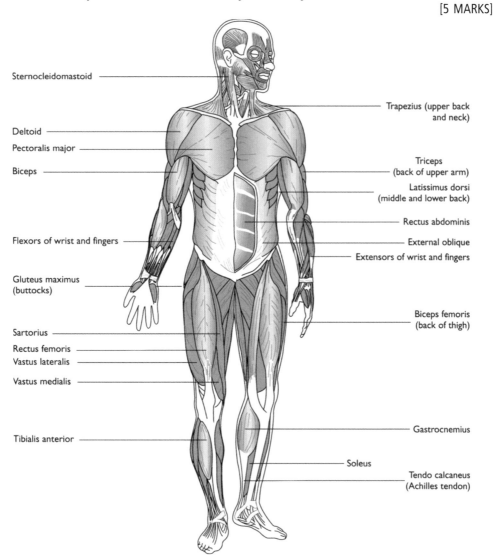

Complete the following sentences by inserting the most appropriate words:

Muscles have the ability to _____ when stimulated by nerves. Almost all movements within the human body, voluntary and involuntary, are caused by muscles, and muscles allow humans to _____ or to get around from one place to another. Muscles are grouped on the basis of structure and function into three types: _____ muscle, _____ muscle and _____ muscle.

[5 MARKS]

5 In the diagram of the human circulatory system shown, label the parts **A** to **J**.

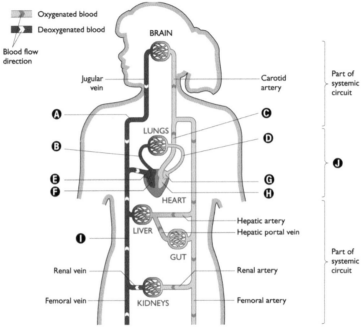

aorta

right ventricle

left ventricle

pulmonary artery

left atrium

right atrium

pulmonary vein

superior vena cava

inferior vena cava

pulmonary circuit

[10 MARKS]

Complete the following sentences by inserting the most appropriate words:

Blood is circulated around the body by the _____ , a four-chambered organ that works like two pumps side by side. The human circulatory system transports _____ , food substances and _____ all around the body. It gets white blood cells and platelets to where they are needed for the fight against _____ and for _____ wounds.

[5 MARKS]

6   In the diagram of the human digestive system shown, label the parts **A** to **M**.

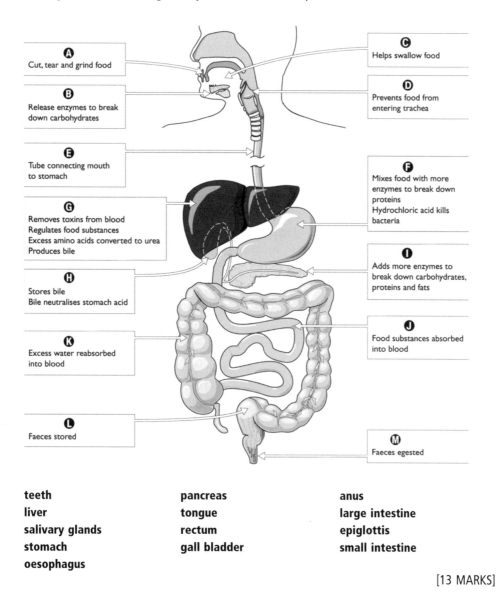

A
Cut, tear and grind food

B
Release enzymes to break
down carbohydrates

E
Tube connecting mouth
to stomach

G
Removes toxins from blood
Regulates food substances
Excess amino acids converted to urea
Produces bile

H
Stores bile
Bile neutralises stomach acid

K
Excess water reabsorbed
into blood

L
Faeces stored

C
Helps swallow food

D
Prevents food from
entering trachea

F
Mixes food with more
enzymes to break down
proteins
Hydrochloric acid kills
bacteria

I
Adds more enzymes to
break down carbohydrates,
proteins and fats

J
Food substances absorbed
into blood

M
Faeces egested

teeth	pancreas	anus
liver	tongue	large intestine
salivary glands	rectum	epiglottis
stomach	gall bladder	small intestine
oesophagus		

[13 MARKS]

Complete the following sentences by inserting the most appropriate words:

The human digestive system essentially receives and, where necessary, processes food into substances that will
_____ . These are eventually transported around the body in the _____ to wherever they are needed.
The processing of food takes place in three stages: _____ , digestion and _____ . During digestion,
which takes place in the digestive tract or _____ canal, the useful constituents or nutrients within food are
released. A _____ diet of _____ , fats, _____ , vitamins, _____ , fibre and water provides
all the nutrients humans need.

[9 MARKS]

7   Draw lines which match the teeth on the left to their function on the right:

incisors		tearing food
canines		crushing and grinding hard food
premolars		cutting food
molars		crushing and grinding soft food

[4 MARKS]

8   Complete the following sentences by inserting the most appropriate words:

Humans reproduce sexually. The _____ fertilisation of a female _____ or sex cell (an egg or ovum) by a male _____ or sex cell (a sperm), usually following sexual intercourse, results in the fusion of cell nuclei and the formation of a _____ containing all of the genetic information or _____ needed in order to produce a fully formed adult. Eventually, and in the uterus, a human _____ grows within its own envir-onment in a fluid-filled sac or amnion which protects it. Here, it gets its oxygen and other useful substances from its mother via the _____ and _____ cord. After a gestation period of about _____ weeks, female humans give birth to babies which grow and mature in order to complete their own life cycles.

[9 MARKS]

9   In common with all other living organisms, humans display certain characteristics which demonstrate that they are alive, and carry out certain processes in order to stay alive. These are frequently represented in the mne-monic **Mrs Gren**. Which life processes are contained within **Mrs Gren**?

[7 MARKS]

10   In the diagram of the generalised human cell shown, label the parts **A** to **E**.

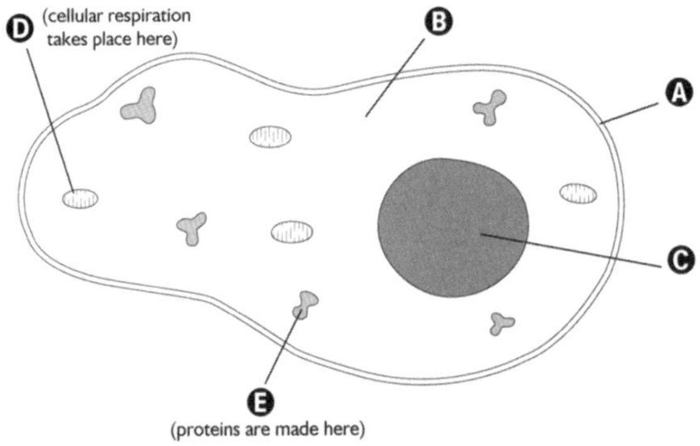

nucleus
cytoplasm
mitochondrion
cell membrane
ribosome

[5 MARKS]

Complete the following sentences by inserting the most appropriate words:

The cell membrane _____ the cytoplasm and nucleus and holds the cell together. Cytoplasm is a jelly-like substance mostly made from _____ . Human cells are eukaryotic. The nucleus contains the cell's genetic material or _____ . The genetic material has the ability to make identical copies of itself in a process known as _____ . Other cell components include mitochondria where glucose and oxygen react during _____ , and ribosomes where _____ are used to make proteins.

[6 MARKS]

11 With reference to the diagrams provided, how are plant and animal cells similar/different?

[2 MARKS]

12 The four main types of pathogen that cause disease in humans are bacteria, viruses, fungi and protoctista. Draw lines which match the pathogens on the left to the types of disease they cause on the right.

| bacteria | | amoebic dysentery, sleeping sickness, malaria |

| viruses | | sore throats, tuberculosis, typhoid, cholera |

| fungi | | athlete's foot, ringworm, thrush |

| protoctista | | colds, flu, measles, mumps, polio |

[4 MARKS]

13 Rearrange the following taxonomic groups in order of size starting with Kingdom.

Kingdom   Species   Order   Genus   Family   Phylum   Class

[1 MARK]

14 In the diagram shown, humans are located within Kingdom Animalia (animals) and Phylum Chordata (chordates). To which of the five major vertebrate classes within Phylum Chordata do humans belong?

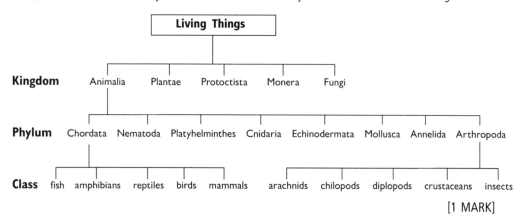

[1 MARK]

15 Common invertebrate organisms are also animals. Draw lines which match the invertebrate animals on the left to their correct taxonomic group on the right.

woodlice		arachnids
worms		molluscs
spiders		crustaceans
snails		insects
butterflies		annelids

[5 MARKS]

29

Continuity and change

1 Define the following terms:

species   **inheritance**

variation   **mutation**

clone

[5 MARKS]

2 Rearrange these structures in order of size starting with the smallest.

cell   **gene**   **nucleus**   **chromosome**

[4 MARKS]

3 Complete the following sentences using the most appropriate words:

In classic genetics, the gene is the basic unit of _____ . Genes carry the instructions for different _____ . Genes are, in fact, short lengths of _____ and long lengths of _____ .

[4 MARKS]

4 How many chromosomes would you expect to find in the typical cells of a healthy human male or female:

(a) 46?
(b) 23?
(c) 72?

[1 MARK]

5 How many chromosomes would you expect to find in the typical sex cells or gametes of a healthy human male or female:

(a) 72?
(b) 46?
(c) 23?

[1 MARK]

6 A human male can roll his tongue (genotype Rr) while his female partner cannot (genotype rr). What are the chances of any children they may have being able to roll their tongues:

(a) 1 in 4?
(b) 1 in 2?
(c) 3 in 4?

[1 MARK]

Ecosystems

1 Look at the diagram of the food web shown and complete the following tasks.

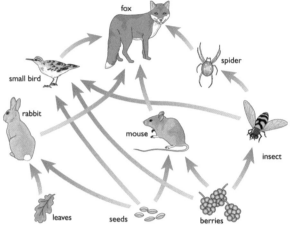

(a) **Name one producer.**

(b) **Name one herbivore and its diet.**

(c) **Name one omnivore and its diet.**

(d) **Name one carnivore and its diet.**

(e) **Write out a complete food chain involving three consumers.**

(f) **What would you expect to happen to the number of foxes if the number of rabbits increased?**

[6 MARKS]

2 Draw lines which match the living organism on the left to its position in a simple food chain on the right.

grass		**primary consumer (herbivore)**
rabbit		**producer**
fox		**secondary consumer (carnivore)**

[3 MARKS]

3 Complete the following sentences using the most appropriate words:

The place where a community of organisms live is called a _____ . A community, together with the living and non-living environmental factors which affect how organisms interact and live their lives, is called an _____ . All living organisms need food for _____ and the raw materials needed for healthy growth. _____ plants are _____ and make their own food by photosynthesis. Animals are _____ and get their food by eating plants and other animals. A food _____ shows how living organisms feed on other living organisms. Complex feeding relationships are better shown using a food _____ . Micro-organisms which feed on the remains of dead plants and animals and return useful chemicals into the soil are known as _____ .

[9 MARKS]

Materials and their properties

Materials including particle theory and the conservation of mass

1 Complete the following sentences by inserting the most appropriate words:

Elements consist of one type of _____ only. There are 92 naturally occurring _____ (there are about 109 in total) and these are grouped according to their similar _____ in the Periodic Table. _____ are formed when two or more substances combine or _____ chemically. _____ are formed when two or more substances are combined physically and the original substances can be _____ relatively easily.

[7 MARKS]

2 In the diagram of the atom shown, label the parts **A** to **C**.

electron

proton

neutron

[3 MARKS]

3 Draw lines which match the particle on the left to its best description on the right.

electron	**a charge of +1 and a mass of 1 amu**
proton	**a charge of −1 and a mass of 1/2000 amu**
neutron	**no charge and a mass of 1 amu**

[3 MARKS]

4 Neutrons and protons make up the nucleus of almost all atoms. True or false?

[1 MARK]

5 The approximate diameter of one atom is:

(a) 0.001mm.
(b) 0.00001mm.
(c) 0.0000001mm.

[1 MARK]

6 With reference to the following symbol:

$$^{16}_{8}O$$

(a) Which element is represented?
(b) What information is given by the number 16?
(c) What information is given by the number 8?

[3 MARKS]

7 Correctly identify each of the following materials as an element, a compound or a mixture:

hydrogen	**air**	**pure water**
ink	**copper**	**carbon dioxide**
sugar	**honey**	

[8 MARKS]

8 Atoms combine with each other in a variety of different ways. The type of bond created determines the properties of the substance formed. The main types of bonding are described below:

Ionic. Atoms donate or receive electrons forming oppositely charged particles called ions; these particles are then strongly attracted to one another forming giant structures.

Covalent. Atoms share electrons with other atoms creating strongly bonded small molecules with weak forces of attraction between the molecules, or atoms share electrons with other atoms creating a giant structure in which all the atoms are strongly bonded together.

Metallic. Free electrons from the outer shell of every atom form a 'sea' around the nuclei of the atoms creating a giant structure.

Draw lines which match the substance on the left to its properties and then on to the type of bonding that exists on the right.

oxygen	**easily soluble in water** **high melting and boiling point** **solution conducts electricity**	**metallic**
copper	**high melting and boiling point** **does not conduct electricity** **insoluble in water**	**covalent (simple molecules)**
diamond	**conducts electricity and heat** **ductile and malleable**	**ionic**
sodium chloride	**low melting and boiling point** **does not conduct electricity** **does not dissolve in water**	**covalent (giant structures)**

[8 MARKS]

9 Materials exhibit different physical properties. Some of these are written in the following table. Fill the table in by selecting from the descriptions and examples provided.

Property	Description	Example
Elastic	_____	_____
Plastic	_____	_____
Hard	_____	_____
Tough	_____	_____
Brittle	_____	_____

Descriptions:

breaks easily

deforms when a force is applied but returns to its original shape when force is removed

is permanently deformed as a result of a force acting on it

does not break or tear easily

very difficult to scratch

Examples:

rubber band

play dough

glass

polythene wrapping

diamond

[10 MARKS]

10 Which of the following statements about physical and chemical changes are *true* and which are *false*?

Physical changes:

(a) are usually reversible.

(b) are usually irreversible.

(c) produce new substances.

(d) cause changes in the arrangement of the particles in a substance.

Chemical changes:

(a) are usually reversible.

(b) are usually irreversible.

(c) produce new substances.

(d) cause changes in the arrangement of the particles in a substance.

[8 MARKS]

11 Draw lines which match the state of matter on the left to its best description on the right.

solid	takes the shape of the container it is in, fixed volume, moderate density, very slightly compressible
liquid	no definite shape, no fixed volume, low density, easily compressible
gas	definite shape, fixed volume, moderate to high density, not compressible

[3 MARKS]

12 In the diagram of the states of matter below, label the changes **A** to **F** which take place between them.

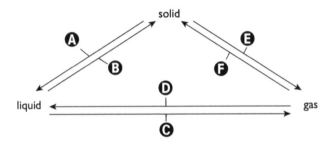

melting	subliming
evaporating/boiling	solidifying/freezing
condensing	reverse subliming

[6 MARKS]

13 Which of the following statements about the change of state of a material from a solid to liquid are **true** and which are **false**?

(a) The particles move faster.
(b) The particles change shape.
(c) The particles lose mass.
(d) The particles move further apart.
(e) The particles gain mass.
(f) The particles have more energy.
(g) The particles are more tightly bonded.

[7 MARKS]

14 When a solid changes to a liquid and then to a gas:

(a) energy is transferred to the molecules of the substance.
(b) energy is released.
(c) no energy is required.

[1 MARK]

15 Correctly identify each of the following as a chemical or a physical change:

Solid carbon dioxide changing into gaseous carbon dioxide.
Ice changing to water.
Paper burning.
A lump of play dough rolled into a 'wiggly worm'.
An egg being boiled.
Sugar dissolving in a cup of coffee.
Salt added to an icy path.
Grass cuttings decomposing in a compost heap.
Concrete hardening.
An iron nail rusting. [10 MARKS]

16 Exothermic reactions occur in chemical reactions when the creation of new bonds requires less energy to form than the bonds that were broken. Endothermic reactions occur in chemical reactions when the creation of new bonds requires more energy than the bonds that were broken. Which of the following examples are exothermic reactions and which are endothermic reactions?

(a) Bicarbonate of soda and vinegar becomes cooler.
(b) Plaster of Paris and water becomes hotter.
(c) Nuclear fission.
(d) Obtaining iron from iron ore. [4 MARKS]

17 When natural gas burns in oxygen the resulting compounds or products are carbon dioxide and water (see the word equation below):

$$\text{methane} + \text{oxygen} \longrightarrow \text{carbon dioxide} + \text{water} + \text{heat}$$

The products would have:

(a) more mass than the reactants.
(b) less mass than the reactants.
(c) the same mass as the reactants. [1 MARK]

18 Draw lines which match the mixture types on the left with the examples on the right.

solid in a solid	air
gas in a liquid	smoke
gas in a gas	Coca Cola
liquid in a gas	clouds
solid in a gas	sand and pebbles
liquid in a liquid	flour in water
solid in a liquid	milk

[7 MARKS]

19 Draw lines which match the mixtures on the left with the examples of separation technique on the right.

paper clips and sawdust	chromatography
pebbles and sand	dissolving, filtering, evaporating
salt and sand	using a magnet
different coloured inks	sieving
water and alcohol	distillation

[5 MARKS]

20 When a salt dissolves in water the salt crystals:

(a) **fill up the spaces between the water molecules.**
(b) **combine with the water to form a new substance.**
(c) **break up and become so small that they are no longer visible.**

[1 MARK]

21 In each of the following examples, identify the solvent, the solute and the solution:

(a) **water, salt, brine.**
(b) **sugar, water, syrup.**
(c) **alcohol, plant oils, perfume.**
(d) **pigment, ink, water.**

[4 MARKS]

22 You smell air freshener almost as soon as it has been sprayed in a room because:

(a) **the molecules of the air freshener travel faster than the molecules of the air.**
(b) **the molecules of the air freshener spread between the molecules of the air.**
(c) **the molecules of the air freshener are smaller than the molecules of the air.**

[1 MARK]

23 Complete the table below using the choices provided.

Rock type	Origin	Examples
Igneous	_____	_____
Metamorphic	_____	_____
Sedimentary	_____	_____

Origin:
   Formed when layers of sediment get buried and crushed under the weight of other layers.
   Formed when heat and pressure completely change existing rocks over long periods of time.
   Formed from the intrusion or extrusion and cooling of molten rock.

Examples:

    Limestone, mudstone, sandstone

    Granite, basalt

    Slate, schist, gneiss, marble

[6 MARKS]

24 Complete the diagram of the water cycle below by labelling the parts **A** to **F**.

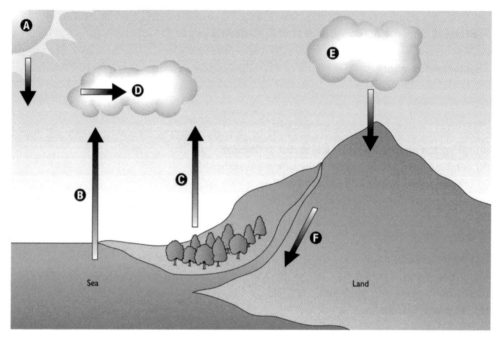

evaporation	**run-off**
precipitation	**heat energy from the Sun**
transpiration	**condensation**

[6 MARKS]

Physical processes

Electricity and magnetism

1 Look at the picture of a simple circuit shown here and complete the following tasks. The filament lamps or bulbs are identical.

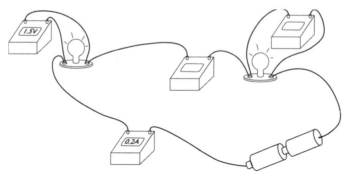

3 volts supplied by battery

(a) This is a series circuit. **True** or **false**?

(b) Underline the most appropriate words in brackets. Unscrewing one bulb from its holder will cause the other bulb to (glow brighter/glow dimmer/glow about the same/go out).

(c) The current flowing in the circuit as shown by one ammeter is 0.2A. What reading would you expect the other ammeter to show?

(d) The voltage (or potential difference) across one of the bulbs as shown by one voltmeter is 1.5V. What reading would you expect the other voltmeter to show?

(e) Use Ohm's Law (V = IR) to calculate the resistance, R, of each of the two bulbs.

(f) Draw a circuit diagram of the picture using standard symbols.

(g) Use the circuit diagram to describe what is happening in the circuit in terms of energy and energy transfer.

(h) Imagine adding a third identical bulb to the circuit. Describe the effect of doing this in terms of bulb brightness.

(i) Draw a circuit diagram which shows the two original bulbs connected in parallel.

(j) With reference to the parallel circuit, how would you expect the bulbs to appear in terms of their brightness compared with the series circuit?

[10 MARKS]

2   In the diagram of the circuit symbols shown, identify the components **A** to **G**.

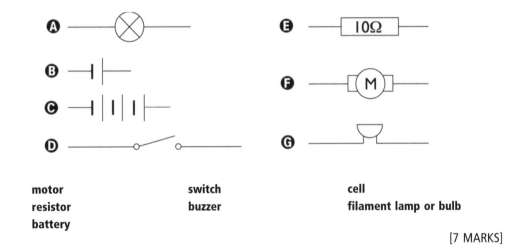

motor	switch	cell
resistor	buzzer	filament lamp or bulb
battery		

[7 MARKS]

3   Define the following terms:

conductor
insulator
current
voltage
resistance
power

[6 MARKS]

4 Under normal circumstances, which of the following materials are good electrical conductors, poor electrical conductors or insulators:

(a) **copper.**

(b) **water.**

(c) **rubber.**

(d) **aluminium.**

(e) **gold.**

(f) **wood.**

(g) **skin.**

(h) **air.**   [8 MARKS]

5 Complete the following sentences by inserting the most appropriate words:

Some materials are magnetic. They are both _____ to magnets and can be _____ . Magnetic materials include the metals _____ and _____ as well as nickel and cobalt. All magnets have _____ and _____ poles. When the poles of magnets are brought close together it is possible to feel an _____ force between them. The rule of magnets states that _____ poles attract while _____ poles repel. A simple compass is nothing more than a freely moving magnet which aligns itself with the Earth's magnetic field. The end of the magnet which points north is referred to as the _____ -seeking pole. The rule of magnets tells us, therefore, that what we refer to as geographical north is actually the Earth's magnetic _____ pole.

[11 MARKS]

6 A simple electromagnet can be made by winding a length of wire around an iron nail. When connected to a battery, a current flows through the wire creating a magnetic field around it. The magnetic field strength is increased by the presence of the nail. List up to three changes that could be made to alter the magnetic field strength of this simple electromagnet.

[3 MARKS]

Energy

1 Energy exists in many different forms. Draw lines which match the form of energy on the left to its best description on the right.

kinetic energy	the energy of vibrating objects
electrical energy	the energy of position or height
heat energy	the energy of being stretched or compressed
light energy	the energy of batteries
sound energy	the energy of hot objects
chemical potential energy	the energy of electromagnetic radiation
gravitational potential energy	the energy of motion and movement
elastic potential energy	the energy of food and fuels

[8 MARKS]

2 Complete the following sentences by inserting the most appropriate words:

A force is a _____ , a _____ , a twist or a turn. In order to exert a force there must be _____ . Without energy and energy transfers, nothing happens and nothing works. Energy can be defined, therefore, as the capacity to make things happen and to do work. Energy is said to be _____ , in other words it is neither created nor destroyed but simply changed or converted from one form to another. Energy can, however, be 'wasted'. When energy is 'wasted' it is said to be _____ . In a torch, for example, _____ energy within the cells is changed or converted to _____ energy which is transferred via wiring to a filament lamp or bulb. Within the filament lamp or bulb, electrical energy is changed or converted to _____ and _____ . One form of energy is useful and helps us to see in the dark, the other is of little real value. The amount of energy available before and after the changes or conversions took place remains the same. Energy is measured in _____ (J).

[10 MARKS]

3 For every 100J of energy transferred to the filament lamp or bulb of a torch, 25J are changed or converted to light while 75J are changed or converted to heat. What is the efficiency of the torch (give your answer as a %)?

[1 MARK]

4 Coal, oil and natural gas are fuels. Fuels are not forms of energy themselves but potential sources of it. Energy can be released from fuels when they are burned. Burning is an irreversible chemical reaction. Coal, oil and natural gas are examples of non-renewable energy sources. What does the term non-renewable used here mean?

[1 MARK]

5 Energy can also be obtained from the Sun, the wind and waves. These are examples of renewable energy resources. What does the term renewable used here mean?

[1 MARK]

6 With reference to the graph showing tea in two different cups cooling over time below:

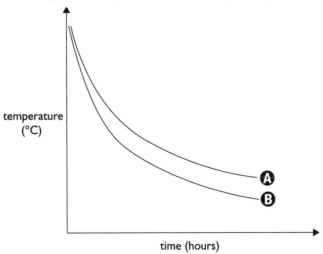

(a) **Which cup keeps the tea hottest for longest, A or B?**

(b) **One cup is made of china and the other polystyrene, which cup is which?**

(c) **Give a reason for your answer.**

(d) **What would happen to the cooling curves if milk were added to the tea?**

(e) **What would happen to the cooling curves if sugar were added to the tea?**

(f) **Explain in energy terms exactly what is happening as the tea cools and the temperature drops. You may wish to consider heat transfers in terms of conduction, convection, radiation and evaporation.**

[6 MARKS]

7 Living things need energy in order to stay alive. This energy is made available during cellular respiration. Cellular respiration requires simple food substances like glucose. Rearrange the following items to produce a word equation for cellular respiration:

glucose
carbon dioxide
oxygen
water
energy

[2 MARKS]

8 Green plants and other photosynthetic organisms are capable of making their own simple food substances like glucose by photosynthesis. Photosynthesis involves a reaction between carbon dioxide and water. Where does the energy come from to drive this reaction?

[1 MARK]

9 Identify the energy changes or conversions in the following diagram of a human at work.

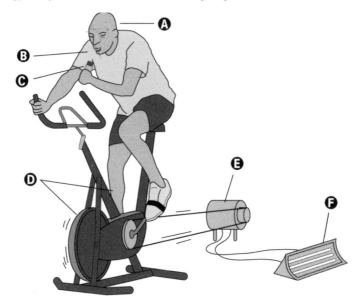

[6 MARKS]

Forces and motion

1 Complete the following sentences by inserting the most appropriate words:

When an object is stationary or moving at a constant speed in a straight line the forces acting on it are said to be _____ . Unbalanced forces cause objects to start moving and _____ up, slow down and come to a stop, or change _____ . Unbalanced forces also bring about changes in _____ . If an object has no _____ force moving it along, it will always slow down and stop because of friction. Friction also includes _____ resistance and _____ resistance. Friction always increases as the speed of a moving object increases. Friction can also be useful. Without friction standing up, riding a bicycle or driving around in cars would be very _____ indeed.

[8 MARKS]

2 Identify and draw, using force arrows, the balanced forces operating in each of the examples below:
(a) a book resting on a table.
(b) a car travelling steadily along a motorway.
(c) an oil tanker at sea.
(d) a jet aircraft cruising at altitude.

[8 MARKS]

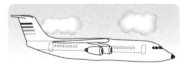

3 Examples of contact forces include:
(a) pushes and pulls.
(b) twists and turns.
(c) all of the above.

[1 MARK]

4 Examples of non-contact forces include:

(a) **gravity and magnetism.**
(b) **electrostatic attraction and repulsion.**
(c) **all of the above.** [1 MARK]

5 In what units are forces measured?

(a) **kilograms (kg).**
(b) **newtons (N).**
(c) **pascals (Pa).** [1 MARK]

6 Describe what you would expect to see happen when a feather and a hammer are dropped from the same height at the same time by a person standing on the surface of the Earth. Describe what you would expect to see happen if the same experiment took place on the surface of the Moon. (This experiment actually took place during one of several Apollo missions to the Moon.)

[2 MARKS]

7 Complete the following sentences by inserting the most appropriate words:

Mass and weight are separate things. The mass of an object is simply the amount of _____ in it. Mass is measured in _____ (kg). The mass of an object remains the same wherever it is in the Universe. Interestingly, any two objects with mass also exert a _____ on each other but this is only noticeable when one of the objects is particularly massive. This force of attraction between all masses is called gravity. Weight is a force. As a result, weight is measured in _____ (N). The weight of an object changes depending on where it is in the Universe. All objects on the surface of the Earth are pulled towards it with a force of about 10 N/kg. The Moon is much less massive than the Earth. All objects on the surface of the Moon are pulled towards it with a force of about 1.6 N/kg. An object on the surface of the Earth therefore weighs _____ than the same object on the surface of the Moon even though it has exactly the _____ mass.

[6 MARKS]

8 The force of gravity on the surface of the Earth is about 10 N/kg. How much would a person of mass 90 kg weigh?

[1 MARK]

9 The force of gravity on the surface of the Moon is about 1.6 N/kg. How much would a person of mass 90 kg weigh?

[1 MARK]

10 Complete the following sentences by inserting the most appropriate words:

The movement of an object can be described in terms of its speed or how _____ it is going. The speed of an object can be calculated easily if we know the _____ it travels and the _____ taken to travel that distance. Speed is usually measured in _____ (m/s). The movement of an object can also be described in terms of its velocity. The term velocity should be used in preference to speed when the _____ in which an object is moving is given. Objects do not always travel at a constant speed or velocity, however. They can always speed up or change direction. Objects which speed up, change direction or do both at the same time are said to _____ .

[6 MARKS]

11 In the middle of a race, a cyclist travels along one 540 m stretch of straight road in 45 seconds. Calculate the speed of the cyclist. At that speed, how long would it take the cyclist to travel a further 120 m? Later in the same race, the cyclist registers a constant speed of 15 m/s for 2 minutes. How far does the cyclist travel in that time?

[3 MARKS]

Light

1 In the diagram of the human eye shown, label the parts **A** to **K**.

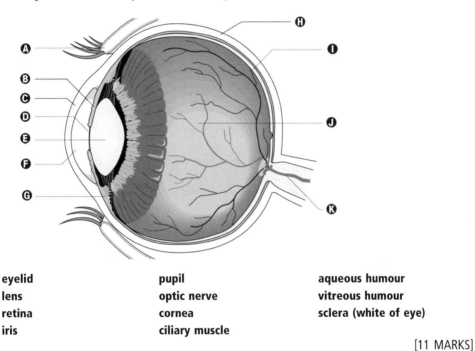

eyelid	**pupil**	**aqueous humour**
lens	**optic nerve**	**vitreous humour**
retina	**cornea**	**sclera (white of eye)**
iris	**ciliary muscle**	

[11 MARKS]

Complete the following sentences by inserting the most appropriate words:

Eyes allow us to see. Each eye has a series of _____ which allow movement within the retaining eye socket. Two eyes provide _____ vision which provides depth perception and distance judgement. Light enters the eye through the cornea and lens which focus the light rays onto a _____ -sensitive layer called the retina. Specialised cells within the retina called _____ (sensitive to colour) and _____ (sensitive to 'greys') change light energy to electrical energy. Electrical impulses travel via the optic nerve to the brain where they are _____ and interpreted as sight. Between the cornea and the lens is the iris. The iris determines the _____ of the eye. At the centre of the iris is the pupil. The pupil changes size in response to the amount of _____ entering the eye.

[8 MARKS]

2   Underline the most appropriate words in brackets.

Short-sightedness or myopia results in light rays being focused 'short' of the retina and within the eyeball itself. This can be corrected using a (converging/diverging) or concave lens. Long-sightedness or hyperopia results in light rays being focused beyond the retina and 'behind' the eyeball itself. This can be corrected using a (converging/diverging) or convex lens.

[2 MARKS]

3   Which of the following sources of light are primary and which are secondary?

(a) A torch.
(b) The Moon.
(c) A burning candle.
(d) The Sun.   [4 MARKS]

4   Light travels in a vacuum at:

(a) 300 000 km/s.
(b) 300 000 m/s.
(c) 300 000 mph.   [1 MARK]

5   Underline the most appropriate word in brackets.

Light travels in waves. These waves are described as (transverse/longitudinal) waves.

[1 MARK]

6   Complete the following sentences by inserting the most appropriate words:

Light is a form of _____ . Light travels in straight lines from a source unless prevented from doing so. Light is a small part of what is referred to as an _____ spectrum of waves which include gamma rays, X-rays, UV, IR, microwaves and radio waves. Light waves have some important features that can be measured: the _____ , which determines the colour of the light, the _____ , or the number of waves that pass every second, and the _____ , which determines the intensity or brightness of the light.

[5 MARKS]

7   The primary colours of light are:

(a) red, blue and yellow.
(b) red, blue and green.
(c) red, green and yellow.   [1 MARK]

8   The primary colours of artists' pigments are:

(a) red, green and yellow.
(b) red, blue and green.
(c) red, blue and yellow.   [1 MARK]

9 A beam of 'white' light passing thr⟨...⟩ ⟨...⟩. This effect is known as dispersion. List the se⟨...⟩ ⟨...⟩ ⟨spectrum⟩ produced.

[1 MARK]

10 The colour of an object is actually the colour or the wavelength of the light it reflects. All other colours or colour wavelengths are absorbed. Why do some objects appear white and others appear black?

[2 MARKS]

11 Underline the most appropriate words in brackets.

Shadows are formed when light is blocked. When the light from a projector is blocked by an object, the shadow formed on a wall, for example, can be made (bigger/smaller) by increasing the distance between the object and the screen or by decreasing the distance between the projector and the object. Some shadows are 'black'. Some shadows appear with a dark central area and a fuzzy, grey outline. The dark part of the shadow is known as the (umbra/penumbra). The fuzzy, grey outline is known as the (umbra/penumbra).

[3 MARKS]

12 Look at the diagram below. Complete the ray diagram to indicate how and where the image of the candle appears to the observer.

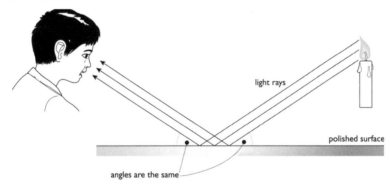

light rays

polished surface

angles are the same

[2 MARKS]

13 Why are polished surfaces better at reflecting light than rough ones?

[1 MARK]

14 Draw lines which match the words on the left with their description on the right.

transparent	blocks light and images completely
translucent	allows light to pass and objects to be seen clearly
opaque	allows light to pass but objects appear blurred

[3 MARKS]

Sound

1 In the diagram of the human ear shown, label the parts **A** to **M**.

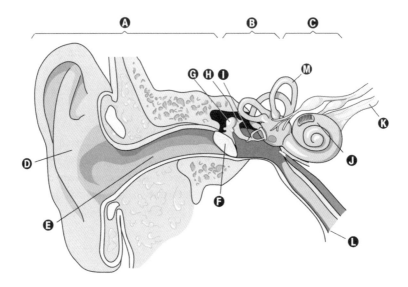

ear drum	**the stirrup**	**pinna**
outer ear	**the hammer**	**auditory nerve**
ear canal	**Eustachian tube**	**middle ear**
cochlea	**inner ear**	**semi-circular canals**
the anvil		

[13 MARKS]

Complete the following sentences by inserting the most appropriate words:

Ears allow us to hear. We have two ears in order to help locate sound sources accurately. Sounds entering the ears cause the ear drums to _____ which in turn force the three small bones of the middle ear to move. Specialised cells within the cochlea (sensitive to vibration and movement) change sound energy to electrical energy. Electrical impulses travel via the auditory nerve to the brain where they are _____ and inter-preted as sound. Unwanted or disagreeable sound is called _____ . Exposure to particularly loud sounds even for short periods of time can damage the ear drum and lead to partial or complete _____ . The ears are never 'switched off'. The Eustachian tube in each ear is responsible for maintaining _____ balance between the middle ear and the outside world. The semi-circular canals are concerned with _____ and orientation and not hearing.

[6 MARKS]

2 Sound travels in air at:

(a) about 330 m/s.
(b) about 330 km/s.
(c) about 330 cm/s.

[1 MARK]

3 Underline the most appropriate word in brackets.

Sounds generally travel (faster/slower) in solids and liquids than in air.

[1 MARK]

4 Underline the most appropriate word in brackets.

Sound travels in waves. These waves are described as (transverse/longitudinal) waves.

[1 MARK]

5 Complete the following sentences by inserting the most appropriate words:

Sound is a form of _____ . Sounds travel outwards from a _____ source in waves. Sounds will travel in solids, liquids and gases but not in a _____ . Some sounds are louder or quieter than others and differ in _____ . Some sounds are higher or lower in pitch than others and differ in _____ . Noise levels are often measured in _____ (dB). Sound waves can also be reflected. Sound reflections are referred to as _____ .

[7 MARKS]

6 Consider the following sources of sound. For each, identify the source of vibration. In the case of the guitar, identify three ways in which the pitch of the sound produced can be changed and one way in which the volume of the sound can be changed.

(a) piano
(b) drum
(c) recorder
(d) guitar   [8 MARKS]

The Earth and beyond

1 Complete the following sentences by inserting the most appropriate words:

The Universe is, quite literally, everything that exists: _____ (from atoms and molecules to stars and galaxies), _____ (visible light together with the rest of the electromagnetic spectrum) and _____ (the vast emptiness within and between galaxies). The Universe is about 12 _____ years old and most probably emerged from an explosive event referred to as the _____ . The Universe has been growing in size or _____ ever since.

[6 MARKS]

2 Complete the following sentences by inserting the most appropriate words:

Galaxies are assemblages of _____ , nebulae and other interstellar materials. A typical galaxy contains about _____ billion stars and measures about _____ light years across. Galaxies are classified into four main groups depending on their appearance: _____ , barred spirals, _____ and irregulars. Galaxies are not randomly scattered throughout the Universe, they occur in clusters: _____ clusters of hundreds or thousands of galaxies and _____ clusters of a few tens. Our own Sun is located within the Orion Arm of what is referred to as the _____ galaxy, one of about 30 other galaxies known as the Local Group.

[8 MARKS]

49

3 Rearrange the following in order of decreasing size starting with the Universe.

Universe	**Earth**	**Milky Way**
Earth–Sun–Moon System	**Moon**	**Sun**
Solar System	**Local Group of galaxies**	

[1 MARK]

4 Draw lines which match the contents of the Solar System on the left to their best description on the right.

Sun	**chunks of ice and other material often seen with a tail**
planets	**natural satellites which orbit planets**
moons	**a star (ball of hot, glowing gas)**
asteroids	**lumps of rock often referred to as minor planets**
comets	**small particles of dust and rock fragments**
meteoroids	**rocky and gassy objects which orbit the Sun**

[6 MARKS]

5 With reference to the Solar System:

(a) List the nine known planets which orbit the Sun in order starting with Mercury.

(b) Which planets are known as the terrestrial or rocky planets?

(c) Which planets are known as the Jovian planets or gas giants?

(d) Mercury, being nearest to the Sun, is the hottest planet. True or false?

(e) Which is the largest planet?

(f) Which planet has the most moons?

(g) Which planets have no moons at all?

(h) Which planets have rings?

(i) The Solar System formed about 4.6 billion years ago. True or false?

[9 MARKS]

6 Correctly label features **A** to **F** of the day and night cycle in the diagram shown.

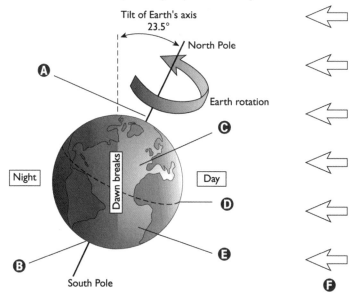

light from the Sun
where more than 12 hours of daylight are experienced
where the Sun never 'rises'
where exactly 12 hours of daylight are experienced
where the Sun never 'sets'
where less than 12 hours of daylight are experienced

[6 MARKS]

7 The day and night cycle is caused by the rotation of the Earth about its axis. The time from one 'sunrise' to the next is:

(a) 24 hours.
(b) 365.25 days.
(c) about one month.

[1 MARK]

8 With reference to the seasons, complete the following sentences by inserting the most appropriate words and by circling the most appropriate words in brackets.

The _____ of the Earth's axis relative to the plane of its orbit around the Sun causes the seasons. In the UK, the year-long cycle of seasons includes spring, summer, autumn and winter . In June, the _____ hemisphere is tilted _____ the Sun and experiences summer while the _____ hemisphere is tilted away and experiences _____ . The effects are dramatic. In the UK, for example, summer days are (long/short), the Sun 'rises' (high/low) above the horizon so the Sun's rays reach the surface of the Earth at a (high/low) angle, and the Earth is (heated/cooled) by the Sun for (more/less) than 12 hours. The Sun's heating effect is (more/less) efficient and summers are warm. In December the opposite occurs.

[11 MARKS]

9 The Earth orbits the Sun once every:

(a) **blue Moon.**
(b) **24 hours.**
(c) **365.25 days.**   [1 MARK]

10 Correctly draw the phases of the Moon as they would be seen from the Earth in the boxes labelled **A** to **H** in the following diagram.

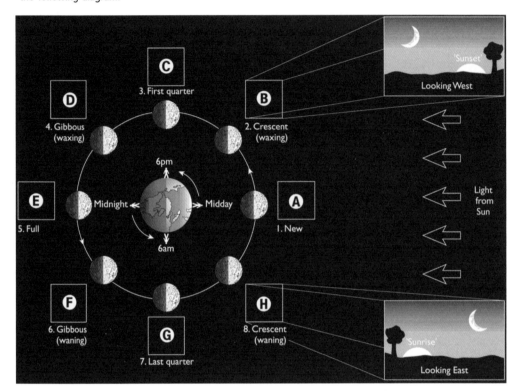

[8 MARKS]

11 The Moon orbits the Earth about:

(a) **once every 24 hours.**
(b) **once a month.**
(c) **once a year.**   [1 MARK]

Making sense of your test results

How well did you do? Determine a separate % score for life processes, materials and their structure and physical processes. Determine an overall score for the test. Remember that your percentage score is relative to the nature of the material tested and the time at which the test took place.

		Score
Life processes	Marks [max 228]	_____ %
Materials and their properties	Marks [max 114]	_____ %
Physical processes	Marks [max 260]	_____ %
Overall	Marks [max 602]	_____ %

Consider the following divisions against which your separate and overall test scores can be measured. The scale is based upon our own experiences of testing trainees in this way over the past few years. It should be used for guidance and relative improvement only and not taken as some sort of absolute test measure.

80–100%   In the areas tested, your score is very good and indicates that you probably exceed the level expected of a non-science specialist. Well done.

60–80%   In the areas tested, your score is good and indicates that you probably meet the level expected of a non-science specialist. Some attention is necessary locally, certainly in the weaker questions. With these marks you probably have little to worry about.

50–60%   In the areas tested, your score is adequate and probably indicates that you are moving towards the level expected of a non-science specialist. However, attention is necessary throughout. Just like perceived competence, you're probably in good company and with a little effort you'll be up there with the best of them.

0–50%   In the areas tested, your score is probably a bit on the low side. But what did you expect? Use the test positively to target the bits you need to work on and really work on them. Remember, you only have to get there by the end of your training. Your score wouldn't concern us at this stage so don't let it concern you.

A useful tip would be to take a break from testing for now. Use the test questions as a guide for some revision. Come back to the test again later and see how much progress you've made.

Part 5: Answers to test questions

Life processes

Functioning of organisms: green plants

1 **A** flower; **B** leaf; **C** stem; **D** tap root; **E** lateral root; **F** root hair; **G** shoot system; **H** root system

Roots **anchor** plants firmly in the ground. They are also responsible for the uptake of **water** and **minerals** from the soil. Stems hold plants upright, spread out leaves for **photosynthesis** and elevate flowers for **pollination**. Most leaves are green due to the presence of **chlorophyll**. Flowers are the structures of most plants which are responsible for **reproduction**.

2 **A** petal; **B** stigma; **C** style; **D** ovary with ovules; **E** anther; **F** filament; **G** sepal; **H** receptacle

Flowers usually consist of five main elements (though these are not always present or immediately obvious): often brightly coloured and scented petals which attract **pollinators**, papery sepals which **protect** the flower in bud, male and female reproductive organs which work together to ensure the **continuity** of each species, and a receptacle which **supports** the weight of everything.

3 (c) the anther and filament

4 (a) the stigma, style and ovary

5 **A** waxy cuticle; **B** upper epidermal cells; **C** palisade mesophyll cells; **D** spongy mesophyll cells; **E** lower epidermal cells; **F** guard cell; **G** stoma; **H** 'vein' (phloem and xylem vessels)

The leaves of many plants are large and **flat** in order to trap sunlight and to make the process of photosynthesis particularly efficient. A cross-section through a leaf blade or **lamina** reveals several layers including one consisting of palisade cells within the palisade mesophyll where most photosynthesis takes place. The rate of photosynthesis is affected by several factors including **light** intensity, air **temperature**, the concentration of **carbon dioxide** in the atmosphere, and **water** availability.

6 (b) autotrophs

7 carbon dioxide + water $\xrightarrow[\text{(chlorophyll)}]{\text{(energy in sunlight)}}$ glucose + oxygen

(*Note*: 1 mark for each side of the equation and 1 mark for sunlight and chlorophyll.)

8 **A** cellulose cell wall; **B** cell membrane; **C** cytoplasm; **D** nucleus; **E** sap-filled vacuole; **F** chloroplast with chlorophyll; **G** ribosome; **H** mitochondrion

The nucleus contains the plant cell's genetic material or **DNA** which ultimately determines what type of cell it is and controls what it does. The genetic material also has the ability to reproduce itself in a process known as **replication**. This is important during cell division as plants **grow**. Chloroplasts contain the green pigment chlorophyll, an important **enzyme** responsible for bringing about photosynthesis.

9 root hair cells   to   take up water and dissolved minerals from soil

guard cells   to   allow various gases to move into and out of leaves

phloem cells   to   form vessels which conduct simple sugars in sap

xylem cells   to   form vessels which conduct water and dissolved minerals

palisade cells   to   carry out photosynthesis in leaves

10 (c) all of the above

11 pollination   to   the transfer of pollen from anther to stigma

fertilisation   to   nuclei of male and female sex cells meet and fuse

seed formation   to   development of embryo plant

seed dispersal   to   scattering mechanism which helps avoid competition

germination   to   appearance of new root and shoot systems

12 (c) all of the above

13 horsetails are sphenophytes

ferns are filicinophytes

flowering plants are angispermophytes (or angiosperms)

mosses and liverworts are bryophytes

club mosses are lycopodophytes

conifers are coniferophytes

14 (a) monocots and dicots

Functioning of organisms: humans and other animals

1 **A** cranium; **B** maxilla; **C** mandible; **D** clavicle; **E** scapula; **F** sternum; **G** rib; **H** humerus; **I** vertebra; **J** ulna; **K** radius; **L** sacrum, ilium and coccyx (bones of the pelvis); **M** femur; **N** patella; **O** fibula; **P** tibia; **Q** carpals, metacarpals and phalanges (bones of the hand); **R** tarsals, metatarsals and phalanges (bones of the foot)

The human skeleton **protects** vital organs. It provides a framework which supports the **weight** of individuals and, with the help of muscles, allows humans to **stand** upright. The human skeleton also provides attachment for **muscles** and **tendons** allowing free movements to take place across joints.

2 (b) 206

3 True

4 (a) The arms bend or flex at the elbow
(b) The arms straighten or extend at the elbow
(c) The gluteus maximus
(d) In the ears
(e) True

Muscles have the ability to **contract** when stimulated by nerves. Almost all movements within the human body, voluntary and involuntary, are caused by muscles, and muscles allow humans to **locomote** or to get around from one place to another. Muscles are grouped on the basis of structure and function into three types: **skeletal** muscle, **smooth** muscle and **cardiac** muscle.

5 **A** superior vena cava; **B** pulmonary artery; **C** aorta; **D** pulmonary vein; **E** right atrium; **F** right ventricle; **G** left atrium; **H** left ventricle; **I** inferior vena cava; **J** pulmonary circuit

Blood is circulated around the body by the **heart**, a four-chambered organ that works like two pumps side by side. The human circulatory system transports **blood**, food substances and **heat** all around the body. It gets white blood cells and platelets to where they are needed for the fight against **disease** and for **healing** wounds.

6 **A** teeth; **B** salivary glands; **C** tongue; **D** epiglottis; **E** oesophagus; **F** stomach; **G** liver; **H** gall bladder; **I** pancreas; **J** small intestine; **K** large intestine; **L** rectum; **M** anus

The human digestive system essentially receives and, where necessary, processes food into substances that will **dissolve**. These are eventually transported around the body in the **blood** to wherever they are needed. The processing of food takes place in three stages: **ingestion** , digestion and **egestion**. During digestion, which takes place in the digestive tract or **alimentary** canal, the useful constituents or nutrients within food are released. A **balanced** diet of **carbohydrates**, fats, **proteins**, vitamins, **minerals**, fibre and water provides all the nutrients humans need.

7 incisors   to   cutting food
   canines   to   tearing food
   premolars   to   crushing and grinding soft food
   molars   to   crushing and grinding hard food

8 Humans reproduce sexually. The **internal** fertilisation of a female **gamete** or sex cell (an egg or ovum) by a male **gamete** or sex cell (a sperm), usually following sexual intercourse, results in the fusion of cell nuclei and the formation of a **zygote** containing all of the genetic information or **DNA** needed in order to produce a fully formed adult. Eventually, and in the uterus, a human **foetus** grows within its own environment in a fluid-filled sac or amnion which protects it. Here, it gets its oxygen and other useful substances from its mother via the **placenta** and **umbilical** cord. After a gestation period of about **40** weeks, female humans give birth to babies which grow and mature in order to complete their own life cycles.

9 **M** movement; **R** reproduction; **S** sensitivity; **G** growth; **R** respiration; **E** excretion; **N** nutrition

10 **A** cell membrane; **B** cytoplasm; **C** nucleus; **D** mitochondrion; **E** ribosome

The cell membrane **encloses** the cytoplasm and nucleus and holds the cell together. Cytoplasm is a jelly-like substance mostly made from **water**. Human cells are eukaryotic. The nucleus contains the cell's genetic material or **DNA**. The genetic material has the ability to make identical copies of itself in a process known as **replication**. Other cell components include mitochondria where glucose and oxygen react during **respiration**, and ribosomes where **amino acids** are used to make proteins.

11 Generally, plant and animal cells both possess a cell membrane, cytoplasm a nucleus and other organelles including mitochondria and ribosomes. Unlike most plant cells, animal cells do not possess a cellulose cell wall, a sap-filled vacuole or, in the case of green tissue plant cells, chloroplasts containing chlorophyll.

12 bacteria   to   sore throats, tuberculosis, typhoid, cholera
viruses   to   colds, flu, measles, mumps, polio
fungi   to   athlete's foot, ringworm, thrush
protoctista   to   amoebic dysentery, sleeping sickness, malaria

13 Kingdom, Phylum, Class, Order, Family, Genus, Species

14 Humans are mammals.

15 woodlice   to   crustaceans
worms   to   annelids
spiders   to   arachnids
snails   to   molluscs
butterflies   to   insects

Continuity and change

1 **Species**: a group of living organisms which share a wide range of common characteristics and can breed together to produce fertile offspring.

Inheritance: those characteristics or features which are received as a result of the genetic make-up of biological parents.

Variation: how living organisms of the same species look or behave differently from each other (could be genetic, e.g. eye colour, or environmental, e.g. as a result of parenting).

Mutation: mutations arise within living organisms as a result of 'faulty' genetic material (some mutations are harmless, some are beneficial and some are harmful).

Clone: identical copies of living things (occurs naturally and artificially).

2 gene, chromosome, nucleus, cell.

3 In classic genetics, the gene is the basic unit of **inheritance**. Genes carry the instructions for different **characteristics**. Genes are, in fact, short lengths of **chromosomes** and long lengths of **DNA**.

4 (a) 46 (as 23 pairs)

5 (c) 23

6 (b) 1 in 2

Ecosystems

1 (a) From the diagram, the leaves, seeds and berries are the 'producers'. Strictly speaking, however, the green plants (e.g. the trees and shrubs) they come from are actually the producers for it is the green plants that produce their own food by photosynthesis and make the leaves, seeds and berries available.

(b) The rabbit is a herbivore, it eats leaves.

(c) The small bird is an omnivore, it eats insects and berries.

(d) The fox is a carnivore, it eats almost all of the other animals present.

(e) berries ⟶ insect ⟶ small bird ⟶ fox

(f) An increase in the number of rabbits potentially provides the foxes with more food. If this situation were to persist, such favourable conditions would support a larger fox population. Fox numbers would therefore be expected to increase too.

2 grass   to   producer

rabbit   to   primary consumer (herbivore)

fox   to   secondary consumer (carnivore)

3 The place where a community of organisms lives is called a **habitat**. A community, together with the living and non-living environmental factors which affect how organisms interact and live their lives, is called an **ecosystem**. All living organisms need food for **energy** and the raw materials needed for healthy growth. **Green** plants are **autotrophs (producers)** and make their own food by photosynthesis. Animals are **heterotrophs (consumers)** and get their food by eating plants and other animals. A food **chain** shows how living organisms feed on other living organisms. Complex feeding relationships are better shown using a food **web**. Micro-organisms which feed on the remains of dead plants and animals and return useful chemicals into the soil are known as **decomposers**.

Materials and their properties

Materials including particle theory and the conservation of mass

1 Elements consist of one type of **atom** only. There are 92 naturally occurring **elements** (there are about 109 in total) and these are grouped according to their similar **properties** in the Periodic Table. **Compounds** are formed when two or more substances combine or **bond** chemically. **Mixtures** are formed when two or more substances are combined physically and the original substances can be **separated** relatively easily.

2 **A** electron; **B** neutron; **C** proton

3 electron   to   a charge of -1 and a mass of 1/2000 amu

proton   to   a charge of $+1$ and a mass of 1 amu

neutron   to   no charge and a mass of 1 amu

4 True

5 (c) 0.0000001 mm

6 (a) oxygen

(b) 16 is the mass number, the total number of protons and neutrons

(c) 8 is the atomic number, the number of protons (and electrons)

7 **Elements**: hydrogen, copper

Compounds: pure water, carbon dioxide, sugar

Mixtures: air, ink, honey

8
oxygen	to	low melting and boiling point	to	covalent (simple molecules)
copper	to	conducts electricity	to	metallic
diamond	to	high melting and boiling point	to	covalent (giant structures)
sodium chloride	to	easily soluble in water	to	ionic

9 Elastic – deforms when a force is applied but returns to its original – rubber band
        shape when force is removed

Plastic – is permanently deformed as a result of a force acting on it – play dough

Hard – very difficult to scratch – diamond

Tough – does not break or tear easily – polythene wrapping

Brittle – breaks easily – glass

10 **Physical changes**: true – usually reversible, cause changes in the arrangement of the particles in a substance; false – usually irreversible, produce new substances

Chemical changes: true – usually irreversible, produce new substances; false – usually reversible, cause changes in the arrangement of the particles in a substance

11 solid   to   definite shape, fixed volume, moderate to high density, not compressible

liquid   to   takes the shape of the container it is in, fixed volume, moderate density, very slightly compressible

gas   to   no definite shape, no fixed volume, low density, easily compressible

12 **A** melting; **B** solidifying/freezing; **C** evaporating/boiling; **D** condensing; **E** subliming; **F** reverse subliming

13 **True**: the particles move faster, the particles move further apart, the particles have more energy

False: the particles change shape, the particles lose mass, the particles gain mass, the particles are more tightly bonded

14 (a) energy is transferred to the molecules of the substance

15 **Chemical change**: paper burning, an egg being boiled, grass cuttings decomposing in a compost heap, concrete hardening, an iron nail rusting

Physical change: solid carbon dioxide changing into gaseous carbon dioxide, ice changing to water, a lump of play dough rolled into a 'wiggly worm', sugar dissolving in a cup of coffee, salt added to an icy path

16 **Exothermic**: plaster of Paris and water becomes hotter, nuclear fission

Endothermic: bicarbonate of soda and vinegar becomes cooler, obtaining iron from iron ore

17 (c) the same mass as the reactants

18 solid in a solid   to   sand and pebbles
    gas in a liquid   to   Coca Cola
    gas in a gas   to   air
    liquid in a gas   to   clouds
    solid in a gas   to   smoke
    liquid in a liquid   to   milk
    solid in a liquid   to   flour in water

19 paper clips and sawdust   to   using a magnet
    pebbles and sand   to   sieving
    salt and sand   to   dissolving, filtering, evaporating
    different coloured inks   to   chromatography
    water and alcohol   to   distillation

20 (c) break up and become so small that they are no longer visible

21 water – solvent, salt – solute, brine – solution
    sugar – solute, water – solvent, syrup – solution
    alcohol – solvent, plant oils – solute, perfume – solution
    pigment – solute, ink – solution, water – solvent

22 (b) the molecules of the air freshener spread between the molecules of the air

23 **igneous** – formed from the intrusion or extrusion and cooling of molten rock – granite, basalt
    metamorphic – formed when heat and pressure completely change existing rocks over long periods of
    time – slate, schist, gneiss, marble
    sedimentary – formed when layers of sediment get buried and crushed under the weight of other layers
    – limestone, mudstone, sandstone

24 **A** heat energy from the Sun; **B** evaporation; **C** transpiration; **D** condensation; **E** precipitation; **F** run-off

Physical processes

Electricity and magnetism

1 (a) True
    (b) Unscrewing one bulb from its holder will cause the other bulb to go out.
    (c) The same current flows through all parts of a series circuit, so 0.2 A.
    (d) The total voltage is shared between components. The bulbs are identical, so 1.5 V.
    (e) Rearranging Ohm's Law gives R = V/I, so R = 1.5/0.2 or 7.5 ohms (the total resistance of the whole circuit
        would be 15 ohms – both bulbs).

(f)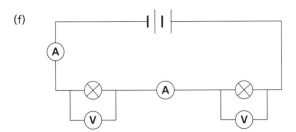

(g) The battery supplies the circuit with electricity and therefore energy. The electrical energy is transferred through the connecting wires to the circuit components, the bulbs, where it is changed or converted to light and heat.

(h) Adding a third bulb increases the resistance of the circuit as a whole. All three bulbs would glow with equal brightness but less brightly than when there were only two.

(i)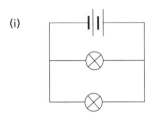

(j) When bulbs are connected in parallel, the overall resistance of the circuit is reduced. Both bulbs would glow with equal brightness but more brightly than in the series circuit.

2 **A** filament lamp or bulb; **B** cell; **C** battery; **D** switch; **E** resistor; **F** motor; **G** buzzer

3 **Conductor**: a material which allows electricity to flow through it

   Insulator: a material which does not allow electricity to flow through it

   Current: the flow of electrons or electricity around a circuit

   Voltage: the energy of the electrical flow (sometimes referred to as the force that pushes the current around)

   Resistance: the difficulty electricity has in passing through a conductor (a resistor is anything that opposes the flow of current)

   Power: the rate at which energy is transferred to, say, a circuit component

4 **Good conductors**: copper, aluminium, gold
   Poor conductors: skin, water
   Insulators: rubber, wood, air

5 Some materials are magnetic. They are both **attracted** to magnets and can be **magnetised**. Magnetic materials include the metals **iron** and **steel (not stainless)** as well as nickel and cobalt. All magnets have **north** and **south** poles. When the poles of magnets are brought close together it is possible to feel an **invisible** force between them. The rule of magnets states that **unlike** poles attract while **like** poles repel. A simple compass is nothing more than a freely moving magnet which aligns itself with the Earth's magnetic field. The end of the magnet which points north is referred to as the **north**-seeking pole. The

rule of magnets tells us, therefore, that what we refer to as geographical north is actually the Earth's magnetic **south** pole.

6 The magnetic field strength can be changed by altering the size of the current flowing through the wire, the number of winds of wire around the nail, and what material the nail is made of.

Energy

1

kinetic energy	to	the energy of motion and movement
electrical energy	to	the energy of batteries
heat energy	to	the energy of hot objects
light energy	to	the energy of electromagnetic radiation
sound energy	to	the energy of vibrating objects
chemical potential energy	to	the energy of food and fuels
gravitational potential energy	to	the energy of position or height
elastic potential energy	to	the energy of being stretched or compressed

2 A force is a **push**, a **pull**, a twist or a turn. In order to exert a force there must be **energy**. Without energy and energy transfers, nothing happens and nothing works. Energy can be defined, therefore, as the capacity to make things happen and to do work. Energy is said to be **conserved**, in other words it is neither created nor destroyed but simply changed or converted from one form to another. Energy can, however, be 'wasted'. When energy is 'wasted' it is said to be **dissipated**. In a torch, for example, **chemical** energy within the cells is changed or converted to **electrical** energy which is transferred via wiring to a filament lamp or bulb. Within the filament lamp or bulb, electrical energy is changed or converted to **light** and **heat**. One form of energy is useful and helps us to see in the dark, the other is of little real value. The amount of energy available before and after the changes or conversions took place remains the same. Energy is measured in **joules** (J).

3 25%

4 Non-renewable means that the energy resources will one day become depleted and cannot ever be used again or replaced.

5 Renewable means that the energy resources will never run out, can be used over and over, and are replaced continually.

6 (a) A
   (b) **A** polystyrene; **B** china
   (c) Polystyrene is a better heat insulator than china. The tea cools more slowly. Alternatively you could say that china is a better heat conductor than polystyrene and the tea cools more quickly.
   (d) The tea would cool rapidly. Both curves would show a marked drop in temperature.
   (e) The tea would cool down but less rapidly than with milk. Both curves would show a marked but gentle drop in temperature.
   (f) Heat energy is transferred through the material of both cups by conduction and radiated into the atmosphere around them. The air around both cups is heated and this energy is transferred further into the atmosphere by convection. Some heat energy is transferred to the atmosphere by evaporation.

7 glucose + oxygen ⟶ carbon dioxide + water + energy

8 The energy which drives photosynthesis comes from the Sun.

9 **A** kinetic to heat; **B** kinetic to sound; **C** chemical to heat and kinetic; **D** kinetic to kinetic; **E** kinetic to electrical; **F** electrical to heat and light

Forces and motion

1 When an object is stationary or moving at a constant speed in a straight line the forces acting on it are said to be **balanced**. Unbalanced forces cause objects to start moving and **speed** up, slow down and come to a stop, or change **direction**. Unbalanced forces also bring about changes in **shape**. If an object has no **driving** force moving it along, it will always slow down and stop because of friction. Friction also includes **air** resistance and **water** resistance. Friction always increases as the speed of a moving object increases. Friction can also be useful. Without friction, standing up, riding a bicycle or driving around in cars would be very **difficult** indeed.

2

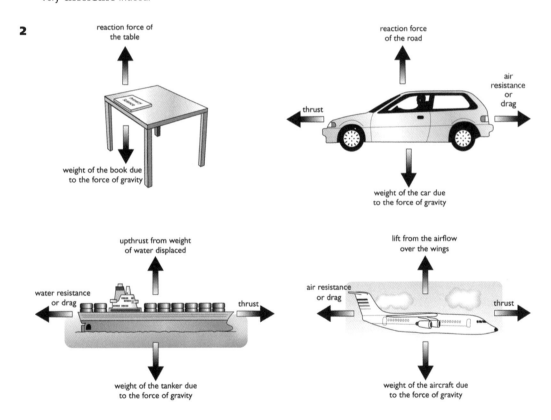

(*Note*: 2 marks for the balanced forces in each example.)

3 (c) all of the above

4 (c) all of the above

5 (b) newtons (N)

6 On the surface of the Earth, the hammer would hit the ground first. The feather would be seriously affected by air resistance which would slow down its fall. On the Moon there is no air. The hammer and the feather would fall together and hit the surface at the same time.

7 Mass and weight are separate things. The mass of an object is simply the amount of **matter** in it. Mass is measured in **kilograms** (kg). The mass of an object remains the same wherever it is in the Universe. Interestingly, any two objects with mass also exert a **force** on each other but this is only noticeable when one of the objects is particularly massive. This force of attraction between all masses is called gravity. Weight is a force. As a result, weight is measured in **newtons** (N). The weight of an object changes depending on where it is in the Universe. All objects on the surface of the Earth are pulled towards it with a force of about 10 N/kg. The Moon is much less massive than the Earth. All objects on the surface of the Moon are pulled towards it with a force of about 1.6 N/kg. An object on the surface of the Earth therefore weighs **more** than the same object on the surface of the Moon even though it has exactly the **same** mass.

8 $10 \times 90 = 900$ N

9 $1.6 \times 90 = 144$ N

10 The movement of an object can be described in terms of its speed or how **fast or quickly** it is going. The speed of an object can be calculated easily if we know the **distance** it travels and the **time** taken to travel that distance. Speed is usually measured in **metres per second** (m/s). The movement of an object can also be described in terms of its velocity. The term velocity should be used in preference to speed when the **direction** in which an object is moving is given. Objects do not always travel at a constant speed or velocity, however. They can always speed up or change direction. Objects which speed up, change direction or do both at the same time are said to **accelerate**.

11 **Speed** = 540/45 = 12 metres per second
Time = 120/12 = 10 seconds
Distance = 15 × 120 = 1800 metres

Light

1 **A** eyelid; **B** iris; **C** cornea; **D** pupil; **E** lens; **F** aqueous humour; **G** ciliary muscle; **H** sclera (white of eye); **I** retina; **J** vitreous humour; **K** optic nerve

Eyes allow us to see. Each eye has a series of **muscles** which allow movement within the retaining eye socket. Two eyes provide **binocular** vision which provides depth perception and distance judgement. Light enters the eye through the cornea and lens which focus the light rays onto a **light**-sensitive layer called the retina. Specialised cells within the retina called **cones** (sensitive to colour) and **rods** (sensitive to 'greys') change light energy to electrical energy. Electrical impulses travel via the optic nerve to the brain where they are **processed** and interpreted as sight. Between the cornea and the lens is the iris. The iris determines the **colour** of the eye. At the centre of the iris is the pupil. The pupil changes size in response to the amount of **light** entering the eye.

2 Short-sightedness or myopia results in light rays being focused 'short' of the retina and within the eyeball itself. This can be corrected using a **diverging** or concave lens. Long-sightedness or hyperopia results in light rays being focused beyond the retina and 'behind' the eyeball itself. This can be corrected using a **converging** or convex lens.

3 **Primary**: a torch, a burning candle, the Sun

  Secondary: the Moon

4 (a) 300 000 km/s

5 Light travels in waves. These waves are described as **transverse** waves.

6 Light is a form of **energy**. Light travels in straight lines from a source unless prevented from doing so. Light is a small part of what is referred to as an **electromagnetic** spectrum of waves which include gamma rays, X-rays, UV, IR, microwaves and radio waves. Light waves have some important features that can be measured: the **wavelength**, which determines the colour of the light, the **frequency**, or the number of waves that pass every second, and the **amplitude**, which determines the intensity or brightness of the light.

7 (b) red, blue and green

8 (c) red, blue and yellow

9 red, orange, yellow, green, blue, indigo and violet

10 Objects which appear white reflect all of the light that falls on them. Objects which appear black absorb all of the light that falls on them.

11 Shadows are formed when light is blocked. When the light from a projector is blocked by an object, the shadow formed on a wall, for example, can be made **bigger** by increasing the distance between the object and the screen or by decreasing the distance between the projector and the object. Some shadows are 'black'. Some shadows appear with a dark central area and a fuzzy, grey outline. The dark part of the shadow is known as the **umbra**. The fuzzy, grey outline is known as the **penumbra**.

12

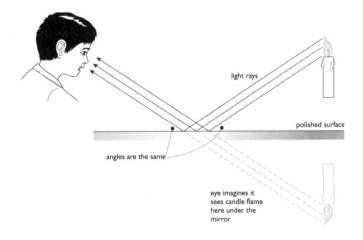

light rays

polished surface

angles are the same

eye imagines it
sees candle flame
here under the
mirror

13 Polished surfaces reflect light perfectly resulting in a clear reflection. Rough surfaces reflect light at different angles resulting in a diffuse reflection.

14 transparent — allows light to pass and objects to be seen clearly
translucent — allows light to pass but objects appear blurred
opaque — blocks light and images completely

Sound

1 **A** outer ear; **B** middle ear; **C** inner ear; **D** pinna; **E** ear canal; **F** ear drum; **G** the hammer; **H** the anvil; **I** the stirrup; **J** cochlea; **K** auditory nerve; **L** Eustachian tube; **M** semi-circular canals

Ears allow us to hear. We have two ears in order to help locate sound sources accurately. Sounds entering the ears cause the ear drums to **vibrate** which in turn force the three small bones of the middle ear to move. Specialised cells within the cochlea (sensitive to vibration and movement) change sound energy to electrical energy. Electrical impulses travel via the auditory nerve to the brain where they are **processed** and interpreted as sound. Unwanted or disagreeable sound is called **noise**. Exposure to particularly loud sounds even for short periods of time can damage the ear drum and lead to partial or complete **deafness**. The ears are never 'switched off'. The Eustachian tube in each ear is responsible for maintaining **pressure** balance between the middle ear and the outside world. The semi-circular canals are concerned with **balance** and orientation and not hearing.

2 (a) about 330 m/s

3 Sounds generally travel **faster** in solids and liquids than in air.

4 Sound travels in waves. These waves are described as **longitudinal** waves.

5 Sound is a form of **energy**. Sounds travel outwards from a **vibrating** source in waves. Sounds will travel in solids, liquids and gases but not in a **vacuum**. Some sounds are louder or quieter than others and differ in **amplitude**. Some sounds are higher or lower in pitch than others and differ in **frequency**. Noise levels are often measured in **decibels** (dB). Sound waves can also be reflected. Sound reflections are referred to as **echoes**.

6 (a) piano – strings struck by key mechanism
(b) drum – skin struck by a drum stick or hand
(c) recorder – air blown into it
(d) guitar – strings plucked or strummed

Pitch can be altered by changing the thickness, the length and the tightness of the strings. Volume can be changed by plucking or strumming with more or less force.

The Earth and beyond

1 The Universe is, quite literally, everything that exists: **matter** (from atoms and molecules to stars and galaxies), **radiation** (visible light together with the rest of the electromagnetic spectrum) and **space** (the vast emptiness within and between galaxies). The Universe is about 12 **billion** years old and most probably emerged from an explosive event referred to as the **Big Bang**. The Universe has been growing in size or **expanding** ever since.

2 Galaxies are assemblages of **stars**, nebulae and other interstellar materials. A typical galaxy contains about **100** billion stars and measures about **100 000** light years across. Galaxies are classified into four main groups depending on their appearance: **spirals**, barred spirals, **ellipticals** and irregulars. Galaxies are not randomly scattered throughout the Universe, they occur in clusters: **rich** clusters of hundreds or thousands of galaxies and **poor** clusters of a few tens. Our own Sun is located within the Orion Arm of what is referred to as the **Milky Way** galaxy, one of about 30 other galaxies known as the Local Group.

3 Universe, Local Group of galaxies, Milky Way, Solar System, Earth–Sun–Moon System, Sun, Earth, Moon

4

Sun	to	a star (ball of hot, glowing gas)
planets	to	rocky and gassy objects which orbit the Sun
moons	to	natural satellites which orbit planets
asteroids	to	lumps of rock often referred to as minor planets
comets	to	chunks of ice and other material often seen with a tail
meteoroids	to	small particles of dust and rock fragments

5 (a) Mercury, Venus, Earth, Mars, Jupiter, Saturn, Uranus, Neptune, Pluto

(b) Mercury, Venus, Earth, Mars

(c) Jupiter, Saturn, Uranus, Neptune

(d) False. Venus is, because of its dense atmosphere and greenhouse effect.

(e) Jupiter

(f) Saturn

(g) Mercury and Venus

(h) Jupiter, Saturn, Uranus, Neptune

(i) True

6 **A** where the Sun never 'sets'; **B** where the Sun never 'rises'; **C** where more than 12 hours of daylight are experienced; **D** where exactly 12 hours of daylight are experienced; **E** where less than 12 hours of daylight are experienced; **F** light from the Sun

7 (a) 24 hours

8 The **tilt** of the Earth's axis relative to the plane of its orbit around the Sun causes the seasons. In the UK, the year-long cycle of seasons includes spring, summer, autumn and winter. In June, the **northern** hemisphere is tilted **towards** the Sun and experiences summer while the **southern** hemisphere is tilted away and experiences **winter**. The effects are dramatic. In the UK, for example, summer days are **long**, the Sun 'rises' **high** above the horizon so the Sun's rays reach the surface of the Earth at a **high** angle, and the Earth is **heated** by the Sun for **more** than 12 hours. The Sun's heating effect is **more** efficient and summers are warm. In December the opposite occurs.

9 (c) 365.25 days

10

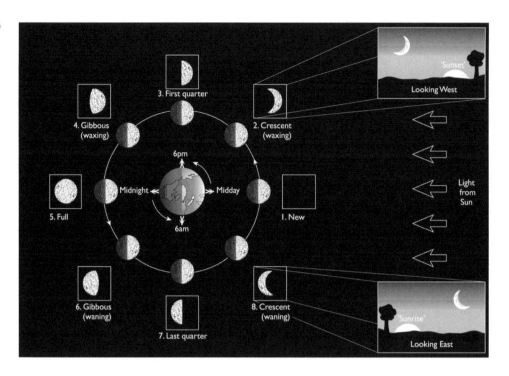

11 (b) once a month

Part 6: Targets for further development

Target setting is an everyday occurrence for most teachers – they do it all the time when assessing and marking children's work and keeping records. Target setting is now seen as a positive step towards helping children make progress. As your own training gets underway, you might well be asked to set targets for yourself. Targets will almost certainly be set for you!

Formally record your targets for further development below (you might need to copy this sheet and make it larger!). Make **clear** and **specific** reference to areas within your perceived competence and science test that require attention. Don't forget to indicate where, when and how the targets will be achieved.

Targets

(areas identified from the audit and test results requiring attention)

Sc2 Life processes	Sc 3 Materials and their properties	Sc4 Physical processes
Functioning of organisms – green plants:	Materials including particle theory and the conservation of mass:	Electricity and magnetism:
Functioning of organisms – humans and other animals:		Energy:
Continuity and change:		Forces and motion:
Ecosystems:		Light:
		Sound:
		The Earth and beyond:

Evidence (record of having achieved targets – nature and location of work undertaken)

Sc2 Life processes	Sc 3 Materials and their properties	Sc4 Physical processes
Functioning of organisms – green plants:	Materials including particle theory and the conservation of mass:	Electricity and magnetism:
Functioning of organisms – humans and other animals:		Energy:
Continuity and change:		Forces and motion:
Ecosystems:		Light:
		Sound:
		The Earth and beyond:

Part 7: Revision and further reading

Well done indeed! Having got this far in the book we can assume that you've managed to work your way through all of the tasks presented. Feeling tired? Take a well earned rest. As we've emphasised throughout, it really doesn't matter how 'well' or how 'badly' you've done: you've already kick-started the process of learning science and at this stage, that's what matters most. It is our experience that many trainees who recognise that they still have some way to go with science actually make very significant progress with a little bit of hard work and effort. It is also our experience that the vast majority of trainees look upon auditing and testing positively and as a valuable step towards QTS.

Recommending which revision guides to use is always something of a challenge. We've already highlighted a text within the *Learning Matters QTS Series* by Johnsey et al. but there are others too and we've listed some below. All have been written with primary trainees and primary teachers in mind and all will be found useful in one way or another. Take a look at a few in your local bookstores before buying one. Read it through and then go back to the test for a second time. We think you'll be amazed at how much better you 'perform'.

Further reading

Farrow, S. (2006) *The Really Useful Science Book*. 3rd ed. London: Falmer.

Hollins, M. and Whitby, V. (2001) *Progression in Primary Science: A Guide to the Nature and Practice of Primary Science at Key Stages 1 and 2*. London: Fulton.

Peacock, G., Sharp, J., Johnsey, R., and Wright, D. (2007) *Primary Science: Knowledge and Understanding*. 3rd ed. Exeter: Learning Matters.

Peacock, G. (2001) *Teaching Science in Primary Schools: A Handbook of Lesson Plans, Knowledge and Teaching Methods*. 2nd ed. London: Letts.

Roden, J., Ritchie, H. and Ward, H. (2007) *Primary Science: Extending Knowledge in Practice*. Exeter: Learning Matters.

Wenham, M. (2004) *Understanding Primary Science: Ideas, Concepts and Explanations*. 2nd ed. London: Paul Chapman.

Online reference sources

Association for Science Education. www.ase.org.uk

BBC learning home page. www.bbc.co.uk/learning

BBC schools home page. www.bbc.co.uk/schools

Sci-centre. www.leicester.ac.uk/education/centres/sci/SCIcentre.html

Virtual Teacher Centre (NGFL). www.vtc.ngfl.gov.uk

(*Note*: Web site addresses are prone to regular change. Use key words in any search engine to track down the sites above.)

Achieving QTS

The Achieving QTS series continues to grow with nearly 50 titles in 8 separate strands. Our titles address issues of teaching and learning across both primary and secondary phases in a highly practical and accessible manner, making each title an invaluable resource for trainee teachers.

Core titles are:

Assessment for Learning and Teaching in Primary Schools (second edition)
Mary Briggs, Angela Woodfield, Cynthia Martin and Peter Swatton
£16   176 pages   ISBN: 978 1 84445 143 2

Assessment for Learning and Teaching in Secondary Schools
Martin Fautley and Jonathan Savage
£16   160 pages   ISBN: 978 1 84445 107 4

Behaviour for Learning in the Primary School
Kate Adams
£13   112 pages   ISBN: 978 1 84445 188 3

Learning and Teaching in Primary Schools
Denis Hayes
£16   168 pages   ISBN: 978 1 84445 202 6

Learning and Teaching in Secondary Schools (third edition)
Viv Ellis
£16   192 pages   ISBN: 978 1 84445 096 1

Learning and Teaching Using ICT in Secondary Schools
John Woollard
£17.50   192 pages   ISBN: 978 1 84445 078 7

Learning to Teach Primary PE
Lawry Price, Ian Pickup, Julie Shaughnessy, Jon Spence and Maxine Trace
£16   160 pages   ISBN: 978 1 84445 142 5

Passing the ICT Skills Test (third edition)
Clive Ferrigan
£8   96 pages   ISBN: 978 1 84445 168 5

Passing the Literacy Skills Test (second edition)
Jim Johnson
£8   80 pages   ISBN: 978 1 84445 167 8

Passing the Numeracy Skills Test (fourth edition)
Mark Patmore,
£8   64 pages   ISBN: 978 1 84445 169 2

Primary English: Audit and Test (third edition)
Doreen Challen
£9   64 pages   ISBN: 978 1 84445 110 4

Primary English: Knowledge and Understanding (fourth edition)
Jane Medwell, George Moore, David Wray and Vivienne Griffiths
£17   240 pages   ISBN: 978 1 84445 274 3

Primary English: Teaching Theory and Practice (fourth edition)
Jane Medwell, David Wray, Hilary Minns, Vivienne Griffiths and Liz Coates
£17   208 pages   ISBN: 978 1 84445 275 0

Primary ICT: Knowledge, Understanding and Practice (third edition)
Jonathan Allen, John Potter, Jane Sharp and Keith Turvey
£16   256 pages   ISBN: 978 1 84445 094 7

Primary Languages: Effective Learning and Teaching
Cynthia Martin
£18   192 pages   ISBN: 978 1 84445 138 8

Primary Mathematics: Audit and Test (third edition)
Claire Mooney and Mike Fletcher
£9   52 pages   ISBN: 978 1 84445 111 1

Primary Mathematics: Knowledge and Understanding (fourth edition)
Claire Mooney, Lindsey Ferrie, Sue Fox, Alice Hansen and Reg Wrathmell
£17   176 pages   ISBN: 978 1 84445 276 7

Primary Mathematics: Teaching Theory and Practice (fourth edition)
Claire Mooney, Mary Briggs, Mike Fletcher, Alice Hansen and Judith McCullouch
£17   192 pages   ISBN: 978 1 84445 277 4

Primary Science: Audit and Test (third edition)
John Sharp and Jenny Byrne
£9   80 pages   ISBN: 978 1 84445 109 8

Primary Science: Knowledge and Understanding (fourth edition)
Graham Peacock, John Sharp, Rob Johnsey and Debbie Wright
£17   224 pages   ISBN: 978 1 84445 278 1

Primary Science: Teaching Theory and Practice (fourth edition)
Rob Johnsey, John Sharp, Graham Peacock, Shirley Simon and Robin Smith
£17   144 pages   ISBN: 978 1 84445 279 6

Professional Studies: Primary and Early Years (third edition)
Kate Jacques and Rob Hyland
£16   256 pages   ISBN: 978 1 84445 095 4

Teaching Design and Technology at Key Stages 1 and 2
Gill Hope
£17   224 pages   ISBN: 978 1 84445 056 5

Teaching Early Years Foundation Stage
Editors: Jo Basford and Elaine Hodson
£16   184 pages   ISBN: 978 1 84445 175 3

Teaching History in Primary Schools
Pat Hoodless
£16   176 pages   ISBN: 978 1 84445 140 1

Teaching Humanities in Primary Schools
Editor: Pat Hoodless
£15   192 pages   ISBN: 978 1 903300 36 7

Teaching Music in Primary Schools
Patrick Jones and Christine Robson
£16   192 pages   ISBN: 978 1 84445 141 8

Teaching Religious Education: Primary and Early Years
Elaine McCreery, Sandra Palmer and Veronica Voiels
£16   176 pages   ISBN: 978 1 84445 108 1

For the full list of titles please see the Learning Matters website www.learningmatters.co.uk

To order please phone our order line 0845 230 9000 or send an official order or cheque to
BEBC, Albion Close, Parkstone, Poole, BH12 3LL
Order online at www.learningmatters.co.uk